Why Literature?

Why Literature?

The Value of Literary Reading and What It Means for Teaching

By
Cristina Vischer Bruns

continuum

2011

The Continuum International Publishing Group
80 Maiden Lane, New York, NY 10038
The Tower Building, 11 York Road, London SE1 7NX

www.continuumbooks.com

Library of Congress Cataloging-in-Publication Data
A catalog record for this book is available from the Library of Congress.

ISBN: HB: 978-1-4411-2520-0
ISBN: PB: 978-1-4411-2465-4

Typeset by Pindar

For Ian, Anna, and Dean

– who are the world to me

Contents

Acknowledgements

Many individuals have played indispensable roles in this book's coming to be, including several who made key contributions in the initial stages of this project. I am indebted to Chris Newfield for his early interest and encouragement; to Giles Gunn for his guidance as I formulated the direction of this inquiry; to Judith Green for her challenging questions that pushed me to ground my inquiry in the experience of real readers; to Gabriele Schwab for introducing me to the thinking that became the heart of this project and for her invaluable critique of its early drafts; and to Sheridan Blau for much engaging conversation about these matters, for indispensable feedback on the work in progress, and for an enthusiasm that fueled my motivation to bring this work to completion. I am grateful to each of them beyond words.

Others have contributed both to the refinement of the manuscript and to my own development as a member of the profession of English studies. Gerald Graff carried on a productive email debate with me about my work that sharpened my thinking and also strengthened my resolve to push forward with the project. Martin Bickman provided a much-needed critique of the manuscript in its later stages. Bruce Novak has given his undying enthusiasm and support for this work. Others have graciously shown interest and offered encouragement as I've sought out guidance along the way, including Rita Felski, David Laurence, James Phelan, Marjorie Perloff, Steve Mailloux, Gene Bell-Villada, John Carlos Rowe, and Peter Rudnytsky.

My colleagues at Chapman University have provided both much-needed advice and a welcoming place to work. I'm especially grateful for timely feedback on portions of the manuscript from Jeanne Gunner and Kevin O'Brien. Of equal importance and meeting an even greater need has been the friendship and encouragement I've received from Justine Van Meter, Ryan Gattis, Brian Glaser, Eileen Jankowski, Alicia Kozameh, Jeff Wallace, and Lacey Walswick. My students at Chapman have also made an essential contribution to this project by taking on with enthusiasm whatever pedagogical experiment I wanted to try out. Their feedback about what we've done together in class has advanced my thinking as much as any other input I've received.

x   Acknowledgements

There are two others who have played valuable roles in this work. Haaris Naqvi at Continuum has supported and shepherded this project, answering my myriad questions through the long publication process. And Deanne Bogdan has demonstrated just how much care and counsel can be conveyed solely through email. Though we have not met in person, she has proved to be a vital source of professional and personal encouragement and wisdom.

Above all, this book would never have come into being without the love and support of my family. My husband Dean and my children, Ian and Anna, are the warm and secure home from which I, their wife and mom, can risk daunting challenges like this one. Without their understanding, love, and support, I would not have been capable of this work.

Preface — Situating the Questioner

Why literature? In most of my years as a reader the question never occurred to me. The importance of literature was to me undeniable. From middle school onward, many of the books in whose worlds I temporarily dwelt — from *The Chronicles of Narnia* to *The Brothers Karamazov* and *King Lear* — provided experiences of such weight and power that I never doubted their significance. Certain poems I encountered in college seemed to take up residence in my mind like familiar fixtures to which I could and did repeatedly return. The process of writing papers on particular literary texts as an English major produced such moving experiences that I still consider my copies of those texts — Toni Morrison's *Song of Solomon*, Thomas Mann's *Doctor Faustus*, T. S. Eliot's *Four Quartets*, among them — to be some of my most cherished possessions. The value of reading literature was, to me, self-evident. None of my pastimes felt more valuable. So why do I raise the question?

Before giving an account of the importance of the question, Why literature?, for the profession of literary study as a whole, I want to establish its significance from my own frame of reference by briefly recounting the occasions in my life which brought me to this inquiry. Donna Haraway provides a justification of sorts for this autobiographical indulgence when she characterizes the typical approaches to the discovery and reporting of knowledge in Western academia as "ways of being nowhere while claiming to see comprehensively", what she calls "the god-trick" (191). The alternative to the god-trick, Haraway asserts, are partial, locatable, situated knowledges, not a view from nowhere but from somewhere. This project, like all works of knowledge, emerges from a particular person in a particular context and to meet a particular need. Rather than leaving those particulars unmentioned, I want to disclose them in order to make explicit the need which motivates this study and the context from which it arises.

Late in my undergraduate years, I stumbled upon another love, nearly able to rival literary reading for my affections: teaching. To satisfy a service requirement, I volunteered as a tutor at the local community college and was surprised by the joy and satisfaction I found in the role. After graduation, with a brand new B. A. in English, a desire to teach, and no credentials, I was hired by an alternative adult education project, initially teaching employment skills to welfare recipients in downtown Chicago and later English as a Second Language in factories for their employees. Not long after taking this job, I was given a copy of Paulo Freire's *Pedagogy of the Oppressed*, the first and, for many years, only book I'd read on education. Under Freire's influence, I learned to see all of my students — long-term welfare recipients and immigrant factory workers — as experts in their own contexts and active contributors to the learning community of the classroom. These rather unconventional teaching environments provided me many rooms full of students with whom I could experiment on different ways to work out what I'd gleaned from Freire's book, particularly how to transfer authority for the production of course content from my shoulders alone as teacher to the students' as co-authors with me. That meant making the objective of the training — in this case, to perform well on a job — the explicit focus of the course and regularly inviting students to think with me about what knowledge and practices were necessary to accomplish that objective. Rather than serving as the sole judge and arbiter of what students needed to know or do, I sought to involve students in creating the content of the course, utilizing the knowledge of the work-world they already possessed and supplementing it with the more specialized knowledge I'd gained from employers.

During those years I also worked on a Masters degree in literature, which eventually enabled me to teach as a community college adjunct. My hope was to teach literature, and so to bring my two favorite pastimes together, but I quickly discovered that all the adjunct jobs were in composition. The seven years I spent developing and refining my own curriculum for employment training and workplace ESL proved to be invaluable experience as I faced a community college composition classroom — with no guidance beyond a short list of textbooks from which to choose. I spent most of the next ten years or so as a part-time community college instructor, developing my own approach to teaching composition by utilizing what I'd learned from Freire and from teaching in those other contexts (and not in resistance to all that's out there about composition pedagogy, but in ignorance of it). Again, I focused as best I could on sharing authority with students in courses that I attempted to construct as joint inquiries (students and me inquiring together), centered on the broad objective of producing effective written work. When asked the purpose of most writing tasks, students routinely pointed to their capacity for communication, which then became the primary criteria by which we evaluated written work. Instead of "good" writing, we focused on writing that communicated effectively. I was able to tap students' vast, though usually tacit, knowledge of communication to involve them in determining the particular criteria by which we would evaluate their written work. As much as I could, I strove to redirect their attention from me as the sole classroom authority to their own (and each others') abilities to recognize effective written communication. Since the classroom apathy common among some of the students I taught could easily undermine the involvement in and ownership of course work necessary to produce this shift in authority, I also sought to counteract that indifference by pushing students early in a course to consider why an ability to write well matters in life and then by attempting to craft assignments that would allow them to experience that value — to experience the power of speaking their minds on paper as they hear the responses of those who read their work, their fellow students and me.

Though I thoroughly enjoyed teaching composition, I didn't forget my hope of eventually teaching literature, and this is where the problem emerged for me. How could I translate the teaching approach I'd developed over my years in composition for a literature classroom? In order to invite students to think with me about what the content of such a course should be, and in order to begin developing an effective course myself, I have to have a clear sense of the objective. What is a literature course attempting to accomplish? And, even more perplexing to me, why does it matter in life? I knew it mattered, or at least I felt it did, but that vague though deeply rooted sense of the value of reading literature seemed inadequate as a guide for my students and me in shaping a course.

My own literary education, as I recall it, offers little help with these questions. I can remember my teachers standing before us in class and speaking, but I can remember little of what any of them said.[1] What I remember most vividly is the power of many of the texts that I read in those classes. A case could be made that this is indeed the point, and that my instructors succeeded in producing a student who could make meaning from literary texts, but who is to say I hadn't developed that ability on my own. What happened in my classes seemed more often to have little connection with the powerful experiences I was having with those texts outside of class.

It would be easiest, it seems, to say that the purpose of a literary education is to enable students to read — or make meaning from — literary

---

1 In my senior year in college I experienced firsthand a challenge of the teaching approach by which I was taught, which may have contributed to my resistance to it. A professor of mine asked me one evening to fill in for her in one of her classes the next morning since she was suffering from laryngitis. She had thought of me since she knew I'd taken the same course with her earlier and would have my notes of her lecture to use. Honored by her request, I agreed, only to find that the notes I'd taken for that particular lecture were less than a page long. It took me approximately eighteen of the fifty minutes of class to speak those notes in as extended a form as I could manage before I dismissed her bemused students early. I had no idea what else to do with them. When she asked me to take her class a second day, I quickly declined, not wishing to relive my embarrassment.

texts, but that claim leaves unanswered a glaring question: what for? Why does it matter that someone can read a work of literature? I could make the assumption that, once my students are able to read literary texts like I can, the value of the endeavor will be self-evident for them as it has been for me. But how can I expect that a course I teach will produce students who've experienced the value of reading literature if I'm unable to conceptualize or articulate that value? Without a conception of that value, how can I ensure that what's done in my classroom fosters experiences of the value of literary reading rather than being merely tangential or, worse yet, an impediment? Instead of merely hoping for the emergence in my students of some nebulous sense of the value of literature, I'm choosing to examine these questions in the form of this project: what is the value of literary reading and how should a conception of that value influence the way we teach literature?

Introduction — the Question and Its Importance

Situating the Question

Why literature? The question is a timely one for the profession of literary study. In the past few decades as marketability and revenue production increasingly take precedence over all other considerations, scholars of the humanities and of literature specifically have faced the need to justify their work. The recent economic downturn has only added to the pressure on English departments.[1] In the words of Sheila Cavanagh, "our famous inability to market ourselves to the world at large is no longer sustainable" (132). Essential for the profession of literary study to flourish or perhaps even to survive is that we articulate more persuasively the value of the work that we do.

Of course, claims for the value of reading and studying literature — works of fiction, poetry, and drama — have been made for millennia, but critiques arising out of deconstruction, cultural studies, and other critical approaches of the past generation, have rendered untenable the assumptions of prior ages. As a result, the challenge of justifying literary study is not only a matter of persuasion but also of conception. Marjorie Perloff makes this distinction in her discussion of the apparent growing irrelevance of the humanities. She claims that solutions offered to this problem tend to construe what's needed as "just a matter of convincing those crass others, whether within the university or outside its walls, that they really need us and can use our products", but the trouble is, according to Perloff, that behind these solutions is the mistaken assumption that "we have a clear sense of what the humanities do and what makes them valuable" (2). In other words, we can't sell the public on what we do until we work out a better understanding of what it is we're doing and why what we do really matters. While the study of literature seems to undergo regular reforms attempting to correct the blind spots of previous generations, including the inclusion in recent decades of minority and underrepresented literatures, these developments have done little

---

1 The most recent Modern Language Association conventions of 2009 and 2011 have devoted numerous sessions to the escalating challenges facing departments of language and literature as universities attempt to address budget shortfalls.

to address the question of literature's value. According to Perloff, ". . . without clear-cut notions of *why* it is worthwhile to read literary texts, whether by established or marginalized writers, in the first place, the study of 'literature' becomes no more than a chore, a way of satisfying distribution requirements" (15 emphasis original).

Perloff's concern that we develop clearer ideas of why it is worthwhile to read literary texts is the objective of this book. Other scholars also share this concern, as is evident by the number of works published in the last decade on the subject of the value of literature.[2] Two distinctions set this book apart from most of these others. One is my explicit intention that the conception of literature's value that emerges from this study resonate with what's commonly called "pleasure reading", or the kind of reading experiences that more likely motivate readers to pick up a work of literature outside of school, an issue to which I'll return later in this introduction. This book's other distinction is that it treats this question ultimately as a pedagogical one. As I explained in the preface, my interest in the value of literature emerged out of my own teaching experience as I struggled to articulate for myself the purpose of a literature course. That the connection be made between our ideas about literature and what we ask of students is crucial for the relevance and effectiveness of the profession. It is, after all, in the classes we teach where we have the greatest opportunity to communicate and even enact our theories of why reading literature is worthwhile. However, evidence suggests that literature instruction may not often succeed at passing on the value of our subject.

Though some students succeed at coming away from their literature courses with an experience of the value of the texts they have read, as I did, many likely consider a literature class to be the "chore" that Perloff describes, like the college student I happened to meet at a wedding reception. He told me that he only had a few courses left before he could graduate, just "crap like literature". When I asked why literature courses were "crap", he contended that all the literature he'd read in school was just a waste of time. The much-discussed National Endowment for the Arts' report, *Reading at Risk*, which showed a marked decline in the reading of fiction and poetry among American adults, suggests that this student's experiences with literature in school are likely more typical than mine. Responsibility for the public's reading habits rests largely on

---

2 These include: Glenn C. Arbery's *Why Literature Matters*, Mark Edmundson's *Why Read?*, Frank Farrell's *Why Does Literature Matter?*, Rita Felski's *Uses of Literature*, Gregory Jusdanis' *Fiction Agonistes: In Defense of Literature*, Mark William Roche's *Why Literature Matters in the 21st Century*, Daniel R. Schwartz's *In Defense of Reading*, Dennis Sumara's *Why Reading Literature in School Still Matters*, and Lisa Zunshine's *Why We Read Fiction*.

schools and universities as the primary locations where these practices are shaped. Writing more than ten years before the NEA study, John Guillory argues, using E. D. Hirsch's terminology, that "if Americans are 'culturally illiterate,' this fact is evidence of the educational system's failure to instill a motive for reading in a nominally literate population" (35). If teachers of literature lack an adequate conception of the value of literary reading, it is unlikely that we will be able to convey to our students why both reading and studying literature is worthwhile. The endeavor then appears to be only one academic task among many, leaving students little motivation to read literary texts outside of school. Perhaps, therefore, the lack of a conception of the value of literary reading is a factor contributing to its apparent marginalization.

While it is impossible to conclusively correlate the findings of the NEA study and an inability of literature courses to instill in students a motive for reading, some teachers of literature have long noticed evidence of inadequacies in literature instruction in their own classrooms. For these teachers, the ineffectiveness of their students' previous literature education has tended to be apparent in the hollowness of students' written work and classroom discussion of texts. According to Sheridan Blau, students in his undergraduate literature courses "behave as if they are obliged to hunt for symbols, . . . engage in perfunctory discussions of prescribed universal themes, or gratuitously compare and contrast characters, rather than address any of the issues that might illuminate a text for a reader who cares about it or account for why a text might be important or interesting or even offensive to real readers" (102).

Writing three decades before Blau, Walter Slatoff makes a remarkably similar observation about his students' dealings with texts: "Many of them learn very well how to bring methods to bear on literary works — how to talk about structures, how to trace themes and patterns of imagery . . . Very few have learned how to bring their experience to bear in such a way as to deepen the work and make it matter" (169). Slatoff's and Blau's students tend so dutifully to perform these mechanical tasks with the texts they're assigned to read, showing little evidence that a text has value for them, because they are trying their best to do with literature what they have been taught to do in their past English classes.

In describing the same kind of pointlessness in students' work that Slatoff and Blau observe, A. D. Moody, of University of York, England, makes explicit the connection between the methods of literature instruction and the work students produce. He writes, ". . . the subtext of their education, if not the overt message, tells [students] that what counts is success in examinations and that nothing succeeds so well as a skillful recycling of some expert's view, while an honest effort to make their own sense of something is unlikely to impress". Moody continues, "The sad consequence is that good students become able to discuss the meaning of a poem without its necessarily meaning anything at all to them. Not infrequently they then reach the cynical conclusion that it is all a meaningless game, poetry and criticism alike" (98). Students' efforts to satisfy their teachers' expectations on exams or in papers preclude their own attempts to make the texts they read meaningful. As a result, according to Moody, Slatoff, and Blau, students learn to perform tasks with literature without experiencing for themselves what makes any of those tasks worthwhile. And this apparent pointlessness of literature courses may not be a phenomenon of only the recent generation. In his history of the academic profession of English, Gerald Graff observes, "By the turn of the century it was a commonplace among educators that English courses were boring or baffling students . . ." (100). The apparent inability of literature courses to instill in students a sense of the value of literature may have already been characteristic of literary study not long after its emergence as an academic field.

Not only is there a lack of an adequate conception of the value of literary reading, but the possibility that students will experience for themselves the practice as worthwhile seems often to be hampered by the mode of instruction — the spoken and unspoken expectations of teachers that constrain and over-determine what students do with a work of literature. This is why this book treats the question of literary value ultimately as a pedagogical one. Students' efforts to satisfy the expectations of their instructors can prevent them from having meaningful experiences reading texts or, at least, may prevent them from bringing into their coursework reports of the meaningful reading experiences they've had outside of class.

This disjunction between literature instruction and the academic field of literary study on one hand, and encounters with literature that readers experience as valuable on the other is worth further examination as it provides focus to this inquiry. Robert Scholes points to the professional priority on specialization as a factor contributing to this gap: "for every move toward greater specialization", he writes, "leads us away from the needs of the majority of our students and drives a larger wedge between our professional lives and our own private needs and concerns" (*Rise and Fall*, 82). When successful scholarship is characterized by increasingly narrow areas of specialization, little room remains in professional practice for attending to the larger questions that can define a field's contribution to society at large. The effect of practicing a profession without remaining mindful of its value in broader life is an inevitable split between the profession and the real needs of those whom the profession serves — both the students and the professors themselves.

A telling and rather dramatic instance of the effect of this exclusion and the split it can produce between professional concerns and private needs is the crisis in professional practice of Jane Tompkins. According to her account in her memoir, *A Life in School: What the Teacher Learned*, it was her education that stifled her love of literature, a loss she struggled to recover later as a professor herself. After describing a childhood and youth spent striving to win approval through her academic performance, Tompkins recounts her memories of pursuing a doctorate in English literature at Yale where "the fear of not wanting to appear stupid or ill-informed was dominant and set the tone". She continues, "People were afraid to show who they really were, and most of all they were afraid to show what had drawn them to study literature in the first place. It was love that had brought us there, students and professors alike, but to listen to us talk you would never have known it" (78–79). Looking back on herself as a student, she sees "a person who was taught not to feel" (212). The banishment of feeling she experienced in graduate school promoted a climate of fear, and it also denied the very quality of literary experience that made her subject of study attractive. The fear and reticence Tompkins develops were not a response to explicit instruction, but to the hidden subtext of classroom interaction — the questions that were asked, the responses that were valued. She was shaped more by the manner of instruction than by its content, a phenomenon she claims is generalizable when she asserts, "The *format* of higher education, its mode of delivery, contains within itself the most powerful teachings students receive during their college years" (212, italics original).

Later in her career, once she'd received tenure at a top institution, Tompkins realized that she no longer needed to be driven by fears of inadequacy and allowed her long-buried feelings to return to both her life and her teaching, with dramatic results. Up to this point, her teaching, she writes, had been "a performance whose true goal was not to help the students learn, as I had thought, but to perform before them in such a way that they would have a good opinion of me" (119). As she rejected that goal, what shaped her teaching instead? She writes, "The desire not to be alone in my classes led to much of what I did by way of experiment. That and the longing to be free from fear. I say that now, in retrospect; at the time I just did things, impelled by a force unnameable" (124). As she felt the freedom to risk laying aside the manner of teaching by which she was taught, all that she initially found to replace it was whatever alleviated the loneliness and fear of her past. And this provided little direction for the teaching of literature, as she acknowledges: "It was as if, given the opportunity to choose between literature and life, or rather, between literature and each other, we chose each other. The class never did learn how to discuss a literary text, though we fell into a habit of reading poetry aloud from time to time" (143). Tompkins rejected the professional practices that preclude meaningful, personal reading experiences, and then struggled to reorient her teaching around the emotional attachment to literary reading that drew her to the profession in the first place.

Not many have responded in the rather drastic manner Tompkins did to the incongruity between the expectations of a literary education and the ways of reading that make the practice both attractive and meaningful, but her case offers an illuminating picture of this peculiar challenge of literary education: teaching in a systematic and academically rigorous way a subject (or a practice) that feels most worthwhile when it takes a deeply personal form. Contributing to this incongruity are instructors' assumptions about the value of literary reading that remain implicit and unexamined, and so are not available to inform the development of instructional methods more conducive to instilling in students a motive for reading. While most teachers likely intend for their students to learn to enjoy literature, the lack of an adequate conception of the value of literary reading may indeed contribute to a preponderance of instructional methods that tend to undermine students' abilities to have experiences with literature whose worth is apparent to them. This study seeks to examine and make explicit the value of the literary reading that avid readers like Tompkins find personally meaningful so that it can serve as a guide for instruction. In this way I hope to begin remedying the split between the academic and the personal.

However it is not only the lack of a conception of literary value that hinders students' opportunities to experience literary reading as worthwhile, but also the scholarly approaches taken toward texts in recent decades which constrain those encounters. Rita Felski points to a source of this problem when she claims, ". . . the current canon of theory yields a paucity of rationales for attending to literary objects" (2), later adding, "our language of critique is far more sophisticated and substantial than our language of justification" (22). An outcome of the current direction of theory in academic literary study is a diminished role for literature, a role Frank Farrell describes as "impoverished". He writes, "To read widely in academic literary criticism of recent decades (that written from 1970 to 2000) is to wonder why literature matters at all" (1). While unquestionably important, the work of deconstruction and cultural criticism leads to an unfortunate result. In Farrell's words, ". . . the arrangements of the literary text itself, the precise way the author has placed particular words in a particular order, seem to lose their importance" (1). According to Farrell's assessment, literature, as it is written about in academic circles, bears little resemblance to the books I and many other readers have found so significant in our lives. With academic criticism's focus on the ways texts are implicated in structures of power or on the undecidability of the meaning of language, the role accorded literary texts in many of these writings does not fit with the reading experiences of those who love literature, those for whom literary reading is of great personal importance. And as these approaches to texts shape what is said and done in literature classrooms, students are further prevented from discovering for themselves "the good of literature". Along with the instructional methods of several generations, the critical approaches dominant in academic literary study in recent decades seem to have little connection to the value many experience in reading literary texts.

The career turn of another well-known literary critic (and, interestingly, a former colleague of Jane Tompkins) serves as an especially vivid instance of the dichotomy between personally meaningful reading experiences and the dominant critical approaches to texts. In his well-known essay, "The Last Will and Testament of an Ex-Literary Critic", Frank Lentricchia explains his choice to abandon the professional practices that brought him success as a literary critic out of frustration at what he considers to be the double life he led. Publicly, as an influential "historian and polemicist of literary theory", he spoke about literature as "a political instrument", but in contrast he describes a secret life in which his "silent encounters with literature are ravishingly pleasurable, like erotic transport" (59). Why did Lentricchia feel that he needed to keep his powerful, personal experiences of reading a secret? He doesn't explore that question except to say, "When I grew up and became a literary critic, I learned to keep silent about the reading experiences of liberation that I'd enjoyed since childhood" (63–64). Lentricchia assumes that the form of literary criticism he learned to practice was incompatible with the form of reading he had loved since childhood, and so the two remained disconnected for him. But rather than allowing his personal reading experiences to cause him to question the dominant critical assumptions about the nature and function of texts, Lentricchia claims he is abandoning professional criticism for personal reading. Because his graduate students have followed the scholarly trend of denying the attraction of reading, Lentricchia says, "I gave up teaching graduate students. I escaped into the undergraduate classroom — in other words, slipped happily underground in order to talk to people who, like me, need to read great literature just as much as they need to eat" (64).[3] In Lentricchia's essay, the dissonance between literary texts as objects for critique and literary texts as sources of deep personal significance could hardly be more blatant, and it remains unresolved and relatively unexamined.

Without a conception of the value of literary reading capable of accounting for personal reading experiences like Lentricchia's and thereby challenging or supplementing the dominant critical approaches of recent decades, he sees no alternative to abandoning professional criticism entirely as if it was necessarily opposed to ways of reading that feel

---

3 The difference between Lentricchia's characterization of his undergraduate students and how Blau, Slatoff, and Moody describe theirs raises questions not only about varieties of student readers, but also about instructors' perspectives of students' experience.

personally valuable. Like Tompkins, Lentricchia rejected the professional practices that can threaten a love of literary reading, though, in his case, not how he taught but whom. In these writings neither Tompkins nor Lentricchia have found a way to integrate the reader and the critic or the reader and the professor. But can't we use the personal to inform the professional? What might Lentricchia's personal reading experiences imply about how literary texts work and toward what effect? What would Tompkins' moving and meaningful encounters with literature suggest for a literary education — what it should seek to accomplish and by what means? These are the questions I want to take up in this study.

Narrowing the Question

The professional crises of Lentricchia and Tompkins serve as illustrative focal points for my inquiry. The benefits of a practice like literary reading are certainly innumerable and widely varied, including, in fact, the importance of the knowledge of human interactions produced by reading literary texts in order to make visible the usually hidden workings of cultural and political power or to demonstrate the indeterminability of language. But this is not the type of value that interests me because this is not what typically motivates readers to pick up a book outside of school, nor is this the type of value that provokes the powerful attachments to certain literary works to which many readers attest. The type of value in literary reading that is my concern is that which Tompkins and Lentricchia sought to regain by their rather atypical professional choices. What is the good of literary reading (and I'm making the assumption that there is one) that is capable of evoking the attraction or compulsion that produces a need to read literature that feels to Lentricchia and his undergraduates like the need to eat? What is the good of literary reading that generates the great love of literature that I've experienced?

Philip Davis offers a memorable description of this kind of interaction with texts as he explains the type of reader that is his concern in his 1992 book, *The Experience of Reading*:

> Not Art for Art's sake, said Lawrence in a letter, but Art for *my* sake. "Reading as if for life", said Dickens of his poor boy David Copperfield. And as it is with these writers, so with the serious reader whom I have in mind. For that is what I am after: the idea of a reader who takes books personally — as if what the book describes had really happened to him or to her, as if the book meant as much to the reader as it had in the mind of the writer behind it.
>
> (22)

Might it be possible to establish a conception of the function of literary reading that renders these personally meaningful reading experiences as significant as they feel? It is this type of value that is capable of setting literary texts apart from other types of texts, a function they serve that other kinds of texts tend not to. It is this type of value that can provide a rationale for sustaining and encouraging the practice of reading literature, that can diminish the conflict between academic literary study and more personally oriented reading, and that can give literature education a greater possibility of fostering in students meaningful encounters with texts that will inspire life-long reading.

The personal significance of encounters with texts has received little acknowledgement in academic circles, perhaps because this aspect of reading seems more self-indulgent than rigorous. While it does apparently ignore the constructedness of texts and the slipperiness of language, reading "for *my* sake" still carries the potential for significant broader social contribution and plays a role in intellectual advances. Self-interest, social good, and intellectual rigor, in this case, need not be considered mutually exclusive. The apparent conflict between the personal, the social and the intellectual underlies the sharp contradiction Frank Farrell points out between conclusions drawn from the work of some figures influential in cultural theory and the motivations that produced such work. In order to more effectively capture Farrell's argument, I will quote him at length:

> More generally, the cultural studies theorist does not see how complicated the process is by which ideas develop and circulate that lead eventually to radical critiques of our forms of life. The recommendation is that we read and write with an awareness of how we are thereby supporting or resisting the role of representations in socially unjust practices. But consider how many of the ideas of cultural studies derived from Foucault and ultimately from Nietzsche. Yet Nietzsche was concerned in his reading and writing with textual energies closely associated with issues of self-formation, of private fears and archaic anxieties, of an aesthetics of self-making that could style itself as healthy and vital. He did reflect on and intervene in systems of social power and subject formation, as in his critique of Christian morality and its sense of innerness. But he did this not to increase the flow of representations less favorable, say, to sexism and colonialisms, but rather to understand his own unhappiness, and his own self-formational needs, as culturally symbolic. A cultural studies theorist placed back in his day would have found him to be considering literature and art in an elitist manner, unconcerned with the marginalizing of the poor. Yet that was the manner in which emerged many ideas that cultural studies as a field finds significant. Another case is that of Melville, whose deeply personal, anxiety-driven meditations on his culture, because of powerful archaic materials in his patterns of self-formation, ultimately led to a richer

critique of the patriarchy and subject formation of his time than did other works that intervened more obviously in public ethical debates. For someone interested in how representations circulate in culture, the cultural studies theorist has an astonishingly impoverished view of how representations emerge that will prove useful to ethical criticism. In teaching students to make only the more direct political readings one may be eliminating the future Nietzsches or Melvilles who might contribute novel ideas to cultural criticism in the future.

(154)

In the cases of Nietszche and Melville, Farrell contends that significant advances in social and cultural theory stemmed not from projects intentionally designed to intervene in public debates but from personally motivated reading and writing, reading and writing that is closer to what Davis describes as a search for "powerfully private moments of echo" (*Experience*, 38), driven by a need more like the need to eat in Lentricchia's comparison, as if one's life depended on it. Farrell then draws a necessary but challenging conclusion: that in emphasizing the political to the exclusion of the personal, teachers may prevent students from performing the kinds of reading and writing that can potentially produce such original contributions.

It is my intention through this project to arrive at an understanding of the value of reading literature that is capable of accounting for these kinds of personally significant experiences with literary texts. In what follows I will examine others' attempts to articulate a conception of literary value, including Farrell's, in order to begin to see what can be said about the value of reading that is unique to literary texts, the benefit of literary reading that is capable of making the endeavor so deeply and personally attractive to many. Following that inquiry, I will return to the question of pedagogy. By working out the implications for our teaching that emerge from the resulting conception of the value of literary reading, I will address the gap scholars like Tompkins, Blau, Slatoff, and Moody recognize between what tends to happen in literature classrooms and the kinds of experiences with literary texts students might consider valuable. By these means I hope both to remedy this need within the profession and to bring some resolution to my own persistent pedagogical question that has arisen out of my teaching experience.

1   Why Read Literature?

The question of literature's value is hardly a new one. Plato himself considered poetry to be in need of defense if it was to be allowed in his republic. Writing several centuries after Plato, Horace provides the terms for the value of poetry that would remain dominant for centuries: that it instructs its readers as well as delights them. The seemingly natural union of moral teaching and pleasure that Horace attributed to literary works, as did generations of critics who followed him, no longer so easily holds together for most who take on the question in recent decades. Conceptions of literature's value put forward today either tend to theorize the good literary reading accomplishes in ways that overlook the nature of pleasurable or satisfying reading experiences, or they tend to articulate aspects of literary pleasures without providing an understanding of the benefit of such experiences, and some benefit is required to justify the practice of literary reading as a human endeavor worth preserving. In this chapter I will examine some recent contributions to the question of the value of literature that exhibit one or the other of these tendencies, and I will then incorporate some additional perspectives on the matter that, I think, together can account for the human benefit of literary reading in a way congruous with the deep satisfactions the practice provides.

Literary Reading as Instructive

A common attempt to justify literature's place as an academic subject is to list skills widely recognized as necessary in today's world that can be developed through reading and writing about texts — skills of interpretation, problem solving, oral and written communication, evidence-based argument, and the ubiquitous critical thinking. While making sense of a literary text even outside of school indeed requires important abilities like making inferences or drawing conclusions, other kinds of texts do as well, so this justification does little to ensure literature's place either in schools or in society. More promising is another common claim: that learning to read literature helps us to read the world around us.

A version of this view is developed in a sophisticated and intriguing way in Lisa Zunshine's book, *Why We Read Fiction*. Drawing on a recent area of research in cognitive psychology called Theory of Mind, Zunshine asserts that reading fiction engages and exercises two broad mental faculties that are essential for social functioning. First is our ability to explain people's behavior in terms of their thoughts, feelings, or beliefs — to recognize the mind behind the action — and second is our ability to keep track of the source of what we are told even through several levels of "embedment" (as in, "She said that he said that you thought . . ."). Making sense of the human world around us requires both of these skills in order to recognize the likely meanings of actions and to identify the reliability of the sources of representations. Reading fiction involves both with varying levels of complexity and so stimulates their use, prompting Zunshine to call one of her chapters, "Why Is Reading a Detective Story a Lot like Lifting Weights at the Gym?" (123). Yet the impulse to pick up a good book may seem quite different than the typical motivation to begin a session of vigorous exercise. Zunshine accounts for the pull of reading, in spite or perhaps because of its calisthenic nature in her view, by claiming that humans crave the kind of social engagement that fiction mimics or represents. For Zunshine, ". . . the novel feeds the powerful, representation-hungry complex of cognitive adaptations whose very condition of being is a constant social stimulation . . ." (10). In other words, literary reading brings pleasure because humans need and enjoy the engagement of these cognitive faculties.

However, this view of literature's value seems not to account fully for some readers' interactions with texts, like those described by Farrell, Davis, and Lentricchia as mentioned in the introduction. Does the claim that humans crave this sort of cognitive stimulation sufficiently explain the attraction of literary reading? Using as illustration reading experiences with which I'm most familiar — my own — I do indeed use the skills Zunshine describes as I read, but overwhelmingly the satisfactions which I relish do not seem focused on those activities but on the experiences they help bring about. What grabs hold of me and stays with me is depth of the loss and regret in *King Lear*, or the growing contentment of the protagonist in the second half of Toni Morrison's *Song of Solomon*, or the shock of sudden death in a Flannery O'Connor story, as I experience them while I read. Zunshine not only acknowledges this objection but articulates it herself by means of a hypothetical reader who complains that Theory of Mind does not capture the "instant recognition and heartache" that can be such an important part of one's interaction with a novel (163). Zunshine's response to this complaint is to contend that Theory of Mind encompasses much more than just the few cognitive faculties she has discussed, and that "we are at present a long way off from grasping fully the levels of complexity this engagement entails" (164). She is persuaded that, as this area of cognitive psychology continues to develop, all aspects of a reading experience will eventually be explained by it. While Zunshine is forthright in acknowledging this objection to her position, her perhaps overly optimistic rejoinder points to a potential gap in this view, and it illustrates the first of the two tendencies of recent conceptions of literary value. Theory of Mind succeeds at providing justification for the practice of literary reading as a beneficial means of stimulating crucial social competencies, but that justification in its current form does not sufficiently resonate with the attachment many readers describe for literature. Based on my own interactions with texts, these cognitive skills are a means toward the literary experiences from which I derive a deep sort of pleasure rather than the source themselves of pleasure.

In another conception of the value of literary reading that emphasizes its capacity for instruction or improvement, literature serves as a potential source of values, perspectives, or ways of living that may be better than one's own or those available in present society.[1] An example of this approach is Mark Edmundson's book, *Why Read?*, one of the only recent contributions to the question located explicitly in the context of teaching. Edmundson advocates teaching students to read literature for "truth" because for many people, in his words, "the truth — the circle, the vision of experience — that they've encountered through socialization is inadequate. It doesn't put them into a satisfying relation to experience" (52). The "best repository" for this non-objectivist type of truth, for "better ways to apprehend the world", are the works of poets, novelists, painters, and composers (52). Thus, for Edmundson, the goal of interpreting literary works is to bring forth "the philosophy of life" latent in them (77), and the truth of a work or its value for a reader can be ascertained by asking of it questions like: "Can you live it? Can you put it into action? Can you speak — or adapt — the language of this work, use it to talk to both yourself and others so as to live better? . . . Can it make a difference?" (56). Edmundson's position does indeed make literature matter by giving it an important use in instruction for life, yet it calls for an approach to texts that is tangential to typical ways of reading for pleasure, requiring much additional work of analysis and reflection in order to identify how or whether a literary work might be "lived". This kind of activity may produce a meaningful intellectual engagement with a text, but the experience of, say, undergoing with Odysseus the relief of his long-awaited reunion with Penelope carries value then mainly as it informs the philosophy of life one might draw from the epic. In this case valuing literature for its instructive capacity seems to leave its potential for delight in a subordinate role. For other scholars, however, the delight or pleasure of literary reading alone is sufficient justification of the practice.

---

1 This is also perhaps an overly simplified version of Mark William Roche's position, that literature in its best instances offers "a window onto the absolute," or "onto an ideal sphere," and through this capacity authors and critics alike can "help readers reach the fullness of value inherent in them as persons" (259). However, a conception of literature's value premised on objective idealism raises many questions in the current intellectual climate.

Literary Reading as a Source of Pleasure

Those who focus almost exclusively on the pleasure of reading literature in recent years seem to do so in explicit resistance to the turn in literary study toward the political. Robert Alter's book, *The Pleasure of Reading in an Ideological Age*, is a clear instance of this. Alter challenges the direction of contemporary literary studies which, he claims, makes literature "seem chiefly a battleground of politics" by offering his readers "a systematic invitation to recall again the particular gratifications of the experience of literature" (4), characterizing literature as "high fun" (30). Marjorie Perloff is another who is troubled by the turn in the field away from the literary and toward political concerns. In her essay on the crisis in the humanities, she does not explicitly propose a response to the question of the good of literary reading, but she does suggest a motivation for the practice that, she claims, will return training in reading literature to favor. That motivation? She writes, "Such study, I believe, will come back into favor for the simple reason that, try as one may, one cannot eliminate the sheer jouissance or pleasure of the text" (17). In other words, according to Perloff, the pleasure produced by literary reading will ensure that the decline in this area of study will not continue unabated. And that pleasure seems to be the ultimate good Perloff attributes to literature, according to a statement she made in an interview published in the *Chronicle of Higher Education*. To explain a key difference between her views on poetry and those of Helen Vendler, the subject of the interview, Perloff said, "I don't think art makes one a better person, that literature teaches you the meaning of life. But the sheer pleasure of the text — the sheer joy in all the different values of literature, fictive or poetic — these are the greatest things" (McLemee, A16). For Perloff, the "sheer joy" of literary texts is sufficient justification for their reading and study. Though Alter's perspective on literature and Perloff's are far from identical, both leave me with the same glaring question. How might they delineate the value of the pleasure of the text or the high fun of literature? Without an understanding of the ultimate good of this kind of pleasure, literary reading appears to be little more than a self-indulgent pastime.

Denis Donoghue also appeals to the pleasure of literary reading as the motivation for its practice and as capable of reversing its decline, but his conception of the source of that pleasure goes further than Perloff's toward articulating its value. In his book, *The Practice of Reading*, Donoghue writes, "The pleasure of reading literature arises from the exercise of one's imagination, a going out from one's self toward other lives, other forms of life, past, present, and perhaps future. This denotes its relation to sympathy, fellowship, the spirituality and morality of being human" (75). For Donoghue literary reading brings the reader pleasure because it involves the exercise of her imagination in a way that draws her toward other lives. It is unclear whether Donoghue would locate the source of the reader's sense of pleasure in the use of imagination itself or in the movement toward others that the text makes possible or perhaps in both. But he does make explicit that it is this exercise of imagination with its connection to the spiritual and moral realms, not the pleasure itself that is the good of literary reading, which, like the other arts, he claims, "should provoke me to imagine what it would mean to have a life different from my own" (56). For him this imaginative activity is somehow pleasurable, and this pleasure can motivate the practice of literary reading. But why might we find such pleasure in imagining that we are different?

C. S. Lewis wrote in a prior and very different generation of literary scholarship, but his reflections on the value of literary reading offer some insight into Donoghue's claims — though they predate them — and so they are worth another look. Unlike Donoghue, Lewis considers the pleasure of literary reading to be a good separate from that of imagining being different, rather than arising from it. Pleasure, for Lewis, derives from the form of a text, a text as *Poiema* or something made, appreciating a text as a carefully constructed object of art (132), a sentiment Perloff might share though the two likely appreciate very different sorts of literary objects. But Lewis considers pleasure alone insufficient explanation for the good of literary reading. It is in the content of the literary text, the text as *Logos* (something said), that Lewis locates another good, perhaps for him the primary good of literary reading, and it is here that his comments intersect with and potentially inform Donoghue's. Making allowance for the overly tidy distinction Lewis seems to draw between the form and the content of a text, what is the good Lewis proposes of reading what literature says? In words remarkably similar to Donoghue's, Lewis writes, "The nearest I have yet got to an answer is that we seek an enlargement of our being. We want to be more than ourselves. Each of us by nature sees the whole world from one point of view with a perspective and a selectiveness peculiar to himself . . . we want to see with other eyes, to imagine with other imaginations, to feel with other hearts, as well as with our own" (137). According to both Lewis and Donoghue, we read literature in order to move beyond ourselves, to enter into others' perspectives, but Lewis adds that our search for "an enlargement of our being" is a fundamental human impulse, "to go out of the self, to correct its provincialism and heal its loneliness" (138). In a particularly pithy summary, Lewis writes, "Literary experience heals the wound, without undermining the privilege, of individuality" (140). In other words, we can share in other lives through reading literature without losing a sense of our own separateness. So "a going out from one's self toward other lives" through literary reading may be a source of pleasure, as Donoghue claims, because it is a means to ease loneliness, to experience a sense of connection with others different from ourselves without the risk of a threat to our own individuality.

This conception of the pleasure of literary reading as an outcome of literature's capacity to facilitate an experience of other lives may certainly be more convincing as a rationale in light of the real world challenges we face than is Perloff's conception of literary pleasure as an apparent end in itself. As human society becomes increasingly more global, it seems that a pervasive sense of alienation grows as well, making any practice that might ease loneliness appealing in its provision of comfort. But justifying an academic subject or even just a human practice on the basis of the pleasure it offers — whether that pleasure derives from an appreciation of an elaborately crafted object or from an experience of a connection with other lives — may be a futile endeavor in the face of so many competing pleasures made possible by newly available technologies. If the reading of fiction, poetry, and drama is in decline, it is accompanied by dramatic growth in visually oriented forms of fiction, especially movies and video games, themselves sources of such pleasure that they are widely considered worth the investment of much time and money. It seems that literary pleasure can't currently compete, leaving it as an insufficient rationale for the reading and study of literature.

There is another problem with basing the value of literary reading on the pleasure it provides: encounters with some works of literature affect some readers in ways much more complex than the term "pleasure" can encompass. In explaining why he has chosen to abandon his professional practice of literary criticism for his private love of reading literature, Frank Lentricchia relates his feelings for the literary texts he calls "the real thing", the books that he experiences as deeply affecting. He writes, "I confess to never having been able to get enough of the real thing. I worry incessantly about using up my stash and spending the last years of my life in gloom, having long ago mainlined all the great, veil-piercing books. Great *because* veil-piercing" (63, italics original). Lentricchia's allusions to drug use — using up his "stash" and "mainlin[ing]" books — certainly convey a type of pleasure derived from texts. Yet his description of his relationship with literature reaches beyond Alter's "high fun", for instance. A "fix" for an addict feels less like the pleasure of some elaborate and enjoyable game, and more like the pleasure of breathing, something upon which his very survival seems to depend. And Lentricchia's repeated phrase "veil-piercing", while pointing to a gain in insight that might appeal to many, conveys a force that feels more painful than pleasurable. (A "piercing" of any kind is not comfortable to experience or observe.) For Lentricchia, the reader, literary reading provides not simple pleasure but an unsettling or stripping form of vision or insight into other lives and other worlds, which he nevertheless craves. Literature can disrupt and disturb as well as delight. Not only does an emphasis solely on the pleasure of literary reading seemingly ignore the painful events captured in many texts (something Alter himself acknowledges), but Lentricchia's confession suggests that it may also deny many readers' experience of reading.

It's the typical experiences of common readers, rather than literary professionals, that inform Rita Felski's book, *Uses of Literature*, and this focus leads to a wider range of outcomes or effects from interactions with texts. Her interest is, in her words, "to do justice to how readers respond to the words they encounter, rather than relying on textbook theories or wishful speculations about what reading is supposed to be", although these readers largely remain abstract in her book (17). Felski's contribution is to rehabilitate four terms describing literary experience that the last few decades of literary theory have called into question and discredited. She does not ultimately construct a rationale for reading literature, but she does demonstrate why these categories of experience can motivate reading and are worth the renewed attention of theorists and critics. According to Felski, reading literature can create forms of social knowledge, and produce experiences of enchantment, recognition, and shock. While an enchanting or transporting experience of a literary world is primarily pleasurable, shock tends not to be, and recognizing some aspect of oneself in a text is as likely to be disturbing as reassuring depending on the nature of what one sees.

This variety of effects suggest that we seek encounters with literature for more than just the delight they can provide, but only knowledge carries with it an obvious benefit or value as it can help us better understand the world around us. Regarding the knowledge that can be learned through literature, Felski claims that we can gain "a deeper sense of everyday experiences and the shape of social life", adding that literature can "expand, enlarge, or reorder our sense of how things are" (83). The value of the other three types of experience, like that of literary pleasure itself, lacks such apparent justification. What is the good of being shocked or encountering a moment of recognition or a sense of enchantment? Enchantment, in spite of or perhaps because of its delights — its moments of "rapturous self-forgetting" (55) — has come under criticism for its links to confusion, deception, and loss of control. Felski only briefly attempts to explain the importance of this literary effect when she claims, "Enchantment matters because one reason that people turn to works of art is to be taken out of themselves, to be pulled into an altered state of consciousness" (76). In other words, it matters because we desire and pursue this kind of experience. This explanation of enchantment's importance begs the question of why it is that we seek out such altered states and if they carry any value beyond the momentary diversions they provide. Once again, claims for the value of literature that emphasize pleasure as well as other affective states prompted by interactions with texts seem to lack a conception of the good of these states capable of justifying the practice of literary reading. In what follows I will attempt to remedy this gap by exploring ways of understanding the importance of these effects of reading using three of Felski's categories of literary experience: enchantment, recognition, and shock.

The Varied Effects of Literary Experience and Why They Matter

Shock

The popularity of horror movies and roller coasters suggests that many people find being shocked entertaining, and certainly such voyeuristic or thrill-seeking impulses are engaged by certain types of fiction. But in less titillating forms, experiences of shock can also serve a psychological function suggested by Lentricchia's use of the phrase "veil-piercing" to describe certain literary works. Being taken outside of ourselves through reading may be part of the delight of literature, but at times it can also involve or even require a shock as it disrupts and pushes us beyond the limits of our self-perception. Walter Slatoff offers some insight into this aspect of literary reading in his book, *With Respect to Readers*, though it's from several decades ago. For Slatoff, the reading experience is one often characterized by a sense of disruption or even threat, and this quality is part of what motivates reading (143). He gathers a range of terms typically used for why we read literature: ". . . that it stretches, widens, heightens, deepens, broadens, extends, increases, expands, or enriches one's consciousness or understanding or awareness or experience" (147). Terms like these imply, as Slatoff explains, that "our normal experience and consciousness are limited, circumscribed, and quiescent and that we read largely because we want and need those limits challenged, want our equilibrium disturbed" (148). Seeing in a different way requires having our usual modes of perception challenged or shaken loose, an effect that suffering a shock can accomplish.

Flannery O'Connor's fiction is known for shocking moments of violence that serve a role like this, both for the characters within her stories and for readers as well (as is evident to anyone who walks into a room of undergraduates who have just read "A Good Man Is Hard to Find" for the first time). O'Connor makes that function explicit in an often-quoted statement: "I have found that violence is strangely capable of returning my characters to reality and preparing them to accept their moment of grace. Their heads are so hard that almost nothing else will do the work" (112). Receiving the "grace" O'Connor offers her characters requires that they must first be stripped of their comfortable but obstructive view of themselves and their world. It is likewise for her readers. The Greek tragedists similarly recognized how appalling actions and revelations work to break through clouded and self-assured vision both in their characters and their audience. The uncomfortably and even painfully shocking experiences readers can suffer in the pages of books indeed matter because we want and need to have our limited awareness stretched, and such expansion often requires breaking open or undoing once-settled perspectives. In this way shock can also facilitate the gains in knowledge that Felski attributes to literary reading by opening up the psychological or intellectual space necessary for new insights. Those realizations can be about the world around us, but when they show us aspects of ourselves they offer the literary effect of recognition, another of Felski's categories.

Recognition

Seeing or discovering something of ourselves in a literary work can come with a shock when the resulting insight is troubling or as a relief when we find that some part of our self is shared with another. These experiences of recognition are important for self-knowledge and at times for comfort or consolation, but they can also serve an even more valuable function as the words of texts can give tangible shape to aspects of our own experience that we can't otherwise grasp. Philip Davis provides a compelling explanation of this role. He writes, ". . . it is as though, at times, we find we cannot hold onto, or even recall, a certain way of feeling — an attitude from the opening of which particular possibilities, otherwise unavailable, may follow. Books may re-open the feel of that anterior attitude, nebulous in itself, yet substantiated in the possibilities it subsequently makes available" (*Experience*, 23). For Davis, certain books enable a reader to hold onto or recall an emotional state or stance, important for making that state available to consciousness for thought and reflection which can lead to other possible developments of self-experience and insight.

Davis helpfully offers some illustrations of this kind of reading experience. In one instance he puzzles over the resonance he feels with Frederic Manning's war novel, *Her Privates We*, searching for the source of the sense of familiarity he experiences in it since, as he acknowledges, he is not much interested in war. Instead he probes for memories of experiencing the extreme tension the novel evokes for him, all more ordinary pressures like taking exams or not wanting to join a popular movement in his university days, "ludicrous analogies", he writes, ". . . compared to war, disaster, death, resurrection", but yet having "something in them akin to those big things" (*Experience*, 268). From this attempt to identify the source of the power of this particular literary text for him, Davis draws a tentative conclusion.

But perhaps small memories associate themselves with large events in books because they need, legitimately, some translation in order to do more justice to an experience merely put to shame in ordinary paraphrase before an uncaring audience. It may be that what turns the minor neurosis into the legitimate fear is a sort of extrinsic bad luck: this time, it did happen — usually it does not. When it doesn't come to anything, you forget the anxiety, since it is not realized in the event, or you dismissively blame yourself for feeling it so inappropriately. But the memory stores something of the unused tension.

(Experience, 268–69)

For Davis, then, certain books provide a vehicle capable of opening up access to that tension laying dormant in memory, a sort of emotional residue otherwise lacking a suitable occasion for its felt presence. In a later essay, Davis succinctly articulates this need. He writes, "Readers are those of us who require other people's poems to get into those areas of thoughtful resonance which we often cannot initially summon for ourselves" ("Place", 155). While experiences of recognition through literary reading can simply remind us that we're not alone, they can also bring to conscious awareness latent or forgotten emotional states within us that would otherwise remain unavailable for thought and resolution. Literary recognition, like the experience of shock, can indeed serve a beneficial role beyond the momentary satisfaction or thrill they may provide. The function and benefit of enchantment, however, the last of Felski's categories, is much more complicated to ascertain.

Enchantment

It seems obvious that most avid readers relish the enchantment of literary reading — the delight we experience when we are magically transported to another time and place, another reality, through the words on the page. But the good of such experiences and the human need they meet usually remain obscure. An unexpected source for an exploration of the enchanting quality of literary experience is J. Hillis Miller. In his book, *On Literature*, Miller departs from his influential work as a deconstructionist to examine and attempt to make sense of his childhood reading experiences with one text in particular, *The Swiss Family Robinson*. For Miller that text seemed "a collection of words fallen from the sky", which allowed him "magical access to a pre-existing world of people and their adventures" (14). Informed by this experience, he claims that a literary work is not "an imitation in words of some pre-existing reality but, on the contrary, it is the creation or discovery of a new, supplementary world, a metaworld, a hyper-reality" (18). In an intellectual climate, in part shaped by Miller himself, that tends to question the capacity of language to refer to any reality, the claim that literary texts give access to a "metaworld" may seem far-fetched, and he acknowledges that this notion "does not have much currency these days" (81).[2] Nevertheless he provides a defense for his claim, and he also makes a rather startling assertion for the importance of this function of literary texts when he writes, "Nor would [the notion that literature gives access to a virtual reality] seem, to most people these days, a sufficient justification for reading words said to be literature. Nevertheless, I claim that this is reason enough. Human beings not only have a propensity to dwell in imaginary worlds. They have a positive need to do so" (81). With reasoning that recalls Felski's explanation for why enchantment matters, Miller slides from observing a human propensity to declaring a human need. He implies that, because we seek opportunities to "dwell in imaginary worlds", we therefore need them, offering as additional evidence of this need the contemporary obsession with movies and video games. But, like Felski's claim, Miller's assertion of the value of these experiences stops short. The question he does not address is why human beings have this need. What does dwelling in those other worlds accomplish for us?

A few other theorists do explore possible roles in human life of the opportunity literature provides to be transported to other worlds. For Gregory Jusdanis the importance of literature has to do with the interaction between the real world and a fictional one, specifically that literature "sustains the boundary between fact and fiction", preventing one from folding into the other (62). Preserving that border serves a social benefit, according to Jusdanis, because "it enables us to take a distance from this reality, criticize it, and ultimately change it" (63). However, remaining mindful that a literary world is a fiction, as Jusdanis emphasizes, may not enable us to gain distance from reality because that awareness prevents a reader from being transported to another place. Distance from the empirical world requires temporarily forgetting that the fictional world is a fiction in order to imagine it and "live it" as real while reading. When literary texts can give readers a lived experience of an alternative world, which requires a temporary blurring of the boundary between the fictional and the real, then literature can potentially assist its readers in critiquing the world in which they ordinarily live by pulling them out of it for a time.

While opportunities to gain distance from the world make it possible to critique it, the mental capacity just to imagine alternative possibilities carries benefit as well. Literature, especially narrative, can evoke these possibilities. According to psychologist Jerome Bruner, the artist creates

---

2 Interestingly, though he acknowledges its likely unpopularity, Miller seems to assume a universality for his claim that literary texts offer entry to a virtual reality when he writes of his claim, "It will seem absurd, that is, except to someone who happens to have an unusual gift for reflecting on what happens when he or she reads a literary work" (81).

possible worlds through the "transformation of the ordinary and the conventionally 'given'" (49), capturing what he calls "the anomaly of personhood — its consequential alternativeness" (41–42), that humanness can be understood and depicted in widely different ways. The experience of this alternativeness has the power to "'subjunctivize,' to render the world less fixed, less banal, more susceptible to recreation," and so literature "makes strange, renders the obvious less so, the unknowable less so as well, matters of value more open to reason and intuition" (159). For Bruner, then, the possible worlds a reader encounters in literary texts serve to foster a flexibility of mind necessary to accommodate or encompass the breadth of human possibilities. But Bruner is less than explicit about why this unsettling of certainties matters, why we need to be opened up to the "alternativeness" of human possibility. One can surmise that Bruner's primary concern, underlying his interest in alternativeness and "subjunctivity", is to respond to the rigid thinking and the intolerance of difference that seems responsible for so much conflict and suffering in the world, but Bruner doesn't make such a justification explicit.

What's apparent, though, is that any benefit from the enchantment of literature or from any other aspect of literary experience centers on its effect on readers — the location of the impact or the contact between text and world (since an unread text can have no effect). The alternative worlds into which texts invite us, in J. Hillis Miller's words, "then enter back into the ordinary 'real' world by way of readers whose beliefs and behavior are changed by reading" (20). Miller continues, "We see the world through the literature we read . . . We then act in the real world on the basis of that seeing" (20). Consequently, in the terms of speech act theory, literature exhibits a performative rather than a constative or referential use of words, one which doesn't merely name a state of affairs but a use of words "that makes things happen by way of its readers" (20). The changes prompted by reading a literary text — by seeing the text's world through that text — we experience in moments of shock, recognition, and enchantment, as well as through an experiential form of knowledge. The reader then brings those changes into the real world through her actions.

Though literature can affect the world by way of its readers specifically through the affective experiences that reading facilitates, most other human activities can do likewise. We are changed by much that we do — playing a sport, caring for a child, receiving an unexpected gift. For literary reading to be a practice worth preserving, some capacity or potential must set it apart. Charles Altieri identifies one of these capacities in an essay in which he constructs a rationale for the reading and teaching of lyric poetry. Like Bruner and Miller, Altieri locates the value of literary reading in its effect — in the change it produces or prompts in the reader. Altieri's contribution to what these others have said about the role of literature relates to this distinction between a performative use of language, one that makes things happen, and a constative or referential use. This distinction emerges for Altieri when the reading of a literary text becomes what he calls "voicing", when a reader not only physically sounds out the words of the text but attempts imaginatively to take on its "voice". Altieri considers this "voicing" valuable because, in his words, ". . . there is no better access to other identities, or to who we become because we can take on other identities, than giving ourselves over to a range of speaking voices. Then we are not watching characters on a screen or a stage; we are actually becoming the voices through which they live" (83). Language used in this way enables readers to inhabit other identities for a time, and it stands in sharp contrast to language used for the conveying of knowledge or truths.

Altieri then elaborates on this difference: ". . . between language used primarily as representation — of self or of world — and language used primarily for realization, for composing energies as aspects of a particular relation the psyche can maintain toward the world and toward other people" (83). In other words, when a reader takes on the voice of a literary text, inhabiting it while reading, that reader's "energies" or patterns of attention and feeling are "composed" differently, a temporary re-shaping of that individual's stance or attitude toward the world and others, a trying-on of a new way of being in the world. Language used as representation invites "seeing in" from the reader, but literary texts offer readers an opportunity for "dwelling in" (83–84). The alternative worlds to which literature transports its readers not only remove them temporarily from their own worlds, offering a vision of another reality, but they can also remove them temporarily from their own patterns of relating, from their own voices. Perhaps an evidence of this phenomenon is the common experience of struggling to "get into" a literary work in the first few pages (or sometimes first few chapters) only to find reading become effortless once one has become accustomed to the text's style, its voice. In the semester I spent reading mostly Shakespeare, his language, especially its cadence and sound, became the voice I heard in my head when talking to myself. Other types of activities, like long conversations with a friend or time spent with a particular piece of music or a certain movie, may to some extent also affect the "composing" of "energies", but literary reading accomplishes this in an especially potent way because a text is "voiced" and experienced primarily within oneself. A reader must submit herself to its language in order to recreate its world. And this experience of being taken out of oneself and to a new place is at the heart of the enchantment many readers find in literature. But, to return to my common refrain, why is this experience and the change it can affect actually important for human life and society? The work of one more theorist will take us closer to an answer.

In his book *Why Does Literature Matter?*, Frank Farrell enumerates certain qualities unique to literary texts, texts which he defines as "those in which the way particular words are arranged in a particular order matters greatly" (152). By means of identifying these capacities, he builds a case against the "impoverishment" of what he calls "literary space" (1). This diminishment of literature's role, he claims, is the outcome of the more radical versions of both the linguistic turn and the cultural studies turn in literary theory that reduce texts to the impersonal mechanisms of language or to projections of social power, and result in the impossibility of meaningful communication of any kind. For literature to matter it must retain some relationship to the world and to the selves who write and read it. When such a relationship is allowed, though without denying in more moderate forms the contributions of deconstruction and cultural studies, Farrell demonstrates that literature retains (or regains) a powerful role in human life, and that role is defined by these unique literary capabilities.

All of these qualities that Farrell identifies bear some relevance to this inquiry, but one is especially helpful as it offers a compelling answer to the question of the human importance of taking on other ways of being through literary reading. According to Farrell literary space is "ritualized", in that rituals offer entrance into "a controlled sequence of activities, an already set scheme of performance", with the goal of producing "ultimately, a more satisfying sense of one's relationship to the forces of the cosmos and to one's community" (13). The stability of ritualized practices safely allows contact with forms of earlier psychic or cultural patterns and such contact influences one's relationship to cosmos and community. Literary texts, likewise, invite readers into "a controlled sequence of verbal experiences, of patterns of investment and identification" (13). The orderliness and stability of the sequence of words makes it possible for the reader to have contact with forces or states that might otherwise prove too threatening to the self or are in some way considered intolerable. Farrell describes this capacity for ritual in a specific literary text, *King Lear*.

> Shakespeare arranges the play as a whole as a ritual, a metaphysical one, where the rhythmic power of the lines allows us to hold steady as a space opens out before us that is extraordinarily bleak, where the chance events of a meaningless universe take human errors and inflate their consequences in pain and suffering, where decades of familial closeness break apart into hatreds. We are not, in watching this, hoping for an exorcism ritual that would magically cleanse this world and take away its difficulties; we want instead a linguistic, theatrical ritual whose containing forms give us the courage to let that bleak space open out, to comprehend it for what it is, and to accept it as the way of the universe.

(138)

The "containing forms" of *King Lear*, the play, in a sense, protect its readers or its audience from facing the full force of the bleakness of Lear's universe while still allowing contact with that universe and inviting readers to take on a stance toward it.

While Shakespeare's tragedies enable readers to enter a world unbearably bleak, Farrell argues that the work of other authors, as different as Samuel Beckett and John Updike, gives access to earlier psychic states like those of young childhood when the self's sense of separateness is forming, characterized by a powerful pull toward identification rather than individuation or by fluctuations or ambiguity in the experience of separateness. Farrell uses object relations theory and the work of psychoanalyst D. W. Winnicott to explore this capacity of some literary texts, devoting an entire chapter to a discussion of literature and Winnicott. The work of authors like Beckett and Updike, Farrell claims, effectively translates the "energies of self-formation into linguistic energies" and allows "that ritual regression to earlier psychic spaces by giving the assurance that it can set things in their place in a linguistic pattern that holds itself firm against any gravitational pull" (224). Because of the careful control — the ordered sequence of words — literary texts can make accessible earlier psychic states that would otherwise feel destructive in their pull toward a loss of individuation.

But what is the good of such access? Literary reading makes possible the development of more complex and responsive ways of setting ourselves in relation to the world not just by modeling or displaying such ways but by allowing in the reader a measured return to the psychic stages in which such stances were initially established. The controlled nature of literature — carefully constructed words fixed on paper — creates a secure space as readers inhabit its language and return to an earlier, more formative state that allows re-formation without disintegration. Enchanting or transporting literary reading temporarily blurs the boundaries between fiction and reality, between self and other, between inner and outer experience, and so it calls for readers to enter a state that resembles that of early self-formation in which the boundaries of the self are more malleable. This temporary blurring or softening of these dividing lines allows us to rework our ways of relating across them, enabling us to take on stances more responsive to the world around us. Only by a carefully contained return to earlier states of self-formation, of more fluid self-other boundaries, is such a reworking possible. I contend that this is what we seek out when we pursue experiences of other worlds and other mindsets through literary reading.

This conception of literature's value accomplishes what so many other contributions fail to do: it brings together the powerful appeal of literary reading — being enchanted as we're carried out of ourselves and into another world, experiences often also involving moments of shock and of recognition — with literature's use or benefit, as these experiences make possible reworkings of our relation with the world. The importance of experiences like these render literary reading as vital as it feels for those who, like Lentricchia, need to read like they need to eat. This account of literature's significance can both explain and validate the importance of the love of literature that many proclaim. Readers develop powerful attachments to certain literary texts because their experiences reading those texts have served a valuable psychological function for them. In this conception pleasure is not the ultimate end of literary reading nor tangential to its use, but intrinsic to the process of gaining benefit from reading. Here the delight of literature is tied to its capacity to instruct its readers or, more accurately, to provide its readers opportunities for their own growth. An understanding of self-formation based in object relations theory forms the core of this conception of literature's value, and so further elaboration of this capacity of literary reading requires a closer look at the work of D. W. Winnicott and others using his ideas.

The Mechanism of Literature's Effects and Its Importance: Literature as a Transitional Object

At the heart of object relations theory is what has come to be known as "transitional" space, a middle state between self and world, "an intermediate area of *experiencing*, to which inner reality and external life both contribute" (Winnicott, 2). Winnicott developed this concept as explanation of the means by which infants initially establish their own sense of separateness from the world around them and also their relationship with that world. When the infant can perceive an external object — initially the mother but later other objects of attachment like a teddy bear or security blanket — as if it is her own creation or part of herself, that illusion allows her to experience temporarily this intermediary space between self and world. This transitional space makes it possible for the infant to move from symbiosis to individuation — to begin differentiating between her self and what is other — gradually, without an unbearable experience of sudden separateness. For a period of time an infant needs to be allowed the illusion that this bear or blanket is at the same time "me and not me". Through this means the infant can tolerate beginning to experience herself as separate from the world around her.

Beyond this initial work of infancy, opportunities to return to the transitional area of experiencing are still essential. Winnicott explains ". . . that the task of reality-acceptance is never completed, that no human being is free from the strain of relating inner and outer reality, and that relief from this strain is provided by an intermediate area of experience which is not challenged (arts, religion, etc.)" (13). Temporarily returning to transitional space in adulthood — when the illusion is not challenged but is tolerated that an object or experience is both "me" and "not me" — allows the reformation or adjustment of the boundaries between self and other that were initially established in infancy. This is an on-going work that is crucial to remain responsive to an ever-changing environment. Any engaging and creative activity where one temporarily loses the sense of one's self as separate enables one to enter this intermediary space, whether listening to a piece of music, playing a sport, watching a movie, or participating in a religious ceremony. Winnicott's object relations theory, then, delineates a crucial role for cultural experience — the arts, religion, and all forms of shared imaginative life — in the formation and reformation of the individual's relationship with his environment, the interplay between internal and external worlds.

The importance of this capacity to reshape these boundaries becomes apparent as we consider what these boundaries define. The work of individuation in infancy establishes the initial form of an individual's relationship to others, setting the pattern for interpersonal relationships throughout life. And this process operates not only on an individual level but also on a societal one, as a culture's patterns of parental care shape that culture's patterns of relating to otherness. As Gabriele Schwab explains, when boundaries between cultures are allowed to rigidify, which contributes to a sense of internal coherence, outside pressure increases producing destructive forms of conflict and hostility (*The Mirror*, 45). On the other hand, Schwab claims, ". . . a dynamic, nondestructive or balancing relationship between cultures in contact . . . would require a permanent renegotiation of their mutual boundaries, a process resulting in a different form of inner coherence based not on domination but on flexibility and openness to change" (*The Mirror*, 45). On-going relations between individuals and between cultures require a constant renegotiation of their boundaries, of the conception of the self and of the other. The flexibility required to maintain balance in these relations results from loosening and re-forming self/not-self boundaries that is possible in transitional space.

This blurring of inner and outer worlds produces two specific types of effect. One is that the tangible shape of the activity or object[3] becomes available to give form to inner states of being of the individual — self-states, moods, or ways of being that are unconsciously part of one's self but would otherwise remain inaccessible to conscious awareness, like when a song provokes sudden tears at some unexpected, even uncanny resonance. Gabriele Schwab offers insight into this matter in describing the effect of reading certain literary texts, experiences like the type Rita Felski called "recognition". In an observation strikingly similar to Philip Davis' account of his experience of some texts, as I discussed earlier, Schwab

---

3 To be clear here, my use of the word "object" refers to more than just a tangible item like a favorite book, song, or painting. It can also be an activity through which one engages with the external world.

claims that some works of literature appeal to an "undifferentiated inner state or zone" within the self and transpose or transform that state "into a tangible artistic form". She writes,

> It is as if some unconscious recollection attaches itself to the borrowed shapes of literature in order to transform into something that is truly experienced. When I think of certain of my moods, for example, the best way to characterize them would be to say that they feel like Beckett's *The Lost Ones*. And it is only since discovering Beckett's text that I am able more freely to move in and out of these moods and that they have become a familiar part of myself.
>
> ("Words and Moods", 109)

An object, then, whether a literary text or a symphony performance, can provide a tangible form for an inner state that may be otherwise inaccessible to conscious experience. Essential to this capacity is that we have the freedom to choose objects according to our own desire that may accomplish this function (or that we have not been left insensitive to that desire by various defenses). Then some of the objects we choose — whether a pastime or a painting — serve to give utterance or form to states within ourselves otherwise unavailable to us.

The other effect of transitional experience is that the qualities of the object leave an impact on the individual who engages with them in this in-between space. The objects we choose not only give form and thus access to inner self-states, they also shape those states as they present us with a form or "an integrity" of their own. A choice like spending an afternoon playing football or reading *Moby Dick*, psychoanalyst Christopher Bollas[4] explains, "not only articulates the self (as its expression); it also encounters the self with its own integrity and forces the self to further psychic elaboration" (36). Because the object has a reality of its own — the established rules and techniques of football, for instance, or the printed text of *Moby Dick* with the images and events the text conveys — one meets the object in an encounter which leaves its mark on the self's way of being and adds to one's self-experience. The individual "elaborates" itself, in a process that is largely unconscious, by choosing an object that is both attuned to what resides within the self in order to give it expression or articulation and that also adds to what is there as the self encounters the already-established form of the object. Both of these types of effect result in a changed or even transformed sense of the self, as formerly

---

4 Christopher Bollas has explored the adult use of transitional objects in two fascinating books, one that I cite here, *Being a Character: Psychoanalysis and Self Experience*, and also *The Shadow of the Object: Psychoanalysis of the Unthought Known* (New York: Columbia UP, 1987).

unconscious moods or states become available for self-knowing and as the object or experience encountered in transitional space leaves its imprint upon the self's way of being in the world. The human need for such experiences can produce in us a sense of craving for activities that foster this kind of transitional experience. Of course, the objects that have such an effect upon us are not only those that we seek out, but often we run into them by chance as events and encounters simply happen to us. "Thus", Bollas explains, "we oscillate between thinking ourselves out through the selection of objects that promote inner experience and being thought out, so to speak, by the environment which plays upon the self" (4).

Regardless of how we come to encounter an object, our interaction with it follows four stages according to Bollas, stages I find helpful in understanding this conception of the use of objects and which will prove instrumental in a consideration of literary reading.[5] Bollas's stages are:

1. *I use the object.* When I pick up a book, go to a concert, telephone a friend, I select the object of my choice.
2. *I am played by the object.* At the moment of my use, the particularity specific to the object — its integrity — transforms me, whether it is Bruckner's Eighth Symphony moving me, a novel evoking associations, or a friend persuading me.
3. *I am lost in self experiencing.* The distinction between the subject who uses the object to fulfill his desire and the subject who is played upon by the action of the object is no longer possible. The subject is inside the third area of self-experiencing. His prior self state and the object's simple integrity are both "destroyed" in the experiential synthesis of mutual effect.
4. *I observe the self as an object.* Emerging from self-experiencing proper, the subject considers where he has been. This is the place of the complex self.

(31)

Though movement through these stages might not progress as sequentially nor distinctly as this listing suggests, it delineates the process by which we make use of objects according to Bollas' formulation. We first choose to read a book or we find ourselves in conversation with a friend and are then affected by that book or that friend. At some point in our use of it, we get lost in the experience, losing our distinct self-awareness.

---

5 It is worth noting that term "use" in the psychoanalytic context implies more than in its everyday usage, connoting in this case a mode of relating which makes the object available for a type of unconscious work.

Key to the process is this third stage, those periods of time when an individual releases herself into the experience of the object, temporarily letting go of her sense of herself as separate from the object and immersing herself in it. According to Bollas, the subject must project a part of himself into the object, to invest it with psychic potential, in "a type of erotic action that must be unconscious and one in which the person is not being, as it were, thoughtful," but must be "a rather simplified consciousness, even out of touch with himself for a moment" (22). With a return to self-awareness and differentiation, to being a complex self again, one is able to reflect on the experience of the object, much like one ponders a dream upon awaking. A return to a state of separateness allows for normal functioning, but it is immersion in an activity like literary reading upon which its transitional potential depends.

The importance of an individual's use of objects in transitional space is apparent when one considers what is lost without it. Not only will a deeper self-awareness be less available to her as aspects of her being remain inaccessible, but her way of relating to the world around her will be more rigid and less adaptable without the access these objects provide to earlier states when the boundary between self and other was not yet distinct, access which facilitates the reformation of those boundaries. These objects necessarily evoke or call forth states already residing within the self or there wouldn't be the resonance — the fit — that enables them to take hold within the self. While supplying form to what was formless is certainly a kind of transformation itself, it also makes these once inaccessible parts of the self newly available for transformation, since what can't be reached can't be changed. At the same time these objects also necessarily introduce new elements — new states or stances or moods, to use a term of Schwab's — that provoke change within the self. Transitional objects, then, serve a vital role as tools for self-formation by providing access to a fuller self-awareness or self-experience that makes possible the reworking of our conception of self and other, our relation with the world. It is this role that literary texts are ideally suited to perform.

Since an object can be considered "transitional" by its location in what Winnicott termed the third space between an individual's inner world and the external world, as both self and not-self simultaneously, then a literary text becomes a prime candidate for this position. Louise Rosenblatt first articulated this in-between status of a literary text in her 1938 book, *Literature as Exploration*, and then expanded her treatment of it in 1978's *The Reader, the Text, and the Poem*. Rosenblatt famously conceives of a work of literature as what arises in the transaction between the text (the marks on the page) and the reader, as she explains:

The transaction is basically between the reader and what he senses the words as pointing to. The paradox is that he must call forth from memory of his world what the visual or auditory stimuli symbolize for him, yet he feels the ensuing work as part of the world outside himself. The physical signs of the text enable him to reach through himself and the verbal symbols to something sensed as outside and beyond his own personal world. The boundary between inner and outer world breaks down, and the literary work of art, as so often remarked, leads us into a new world. It becomes part of the experience which we bring to our future encounters in literature and life.

(*Reader*, 21)

The marks on the page, which exist in the external world, are meaningless outside of the mind of a reader who constructs from them the images and events, the meanings, to which they point by calling on her own repertoire of experiences and impressions. In this way, the boundary between the inner and outer worlds drops and a literary text necessarily takes up residence in a third space between them.[6] While all written texts require readers to construct meaning from them, literary texts in particular call upon readers' inner resources to bring into being the worlds they create. A literary work is not of the reader because it comes from outside her, and yet it is of the reader because her mind constructs the images and events (and even the sounds of the words themselves) under the guidance of the marks on the page.

Another feature of literature that makes it conducive to use in transitional space is that these texts, more than other uses of language, emphasize form as well as content, enabling them to convey a sense of voice. As I discussed earlier, taking on the voice of a literary text gives readers opportunity to inhabit another way of being in the world, but the ways literary language captures what Schwab calls a "voice-feeling" — rhythms, tonality, pace, the sounds of language — also recall our earliest experiences of language. Schwab observes that these are the very qualities of language that we perceive before we acquire a symbolic system of meanings so that "they are particularly prone to carrying mnemonic resonances with the wordless worlds which contain our earliest 'grammar

---

6 Yet a literary text can manipulate the reader's sense of distance from it by making more or less apparent to the reader the efforts required of him to make a world from its words. Gabriele Schwab observes that texts "may pull us in so strongly that we feel we merge with their imaginary voices or worlds, or they may hold us at a distance, forcing us consciously to apprehend the performative operations and formal construction of poetic language" ("Cultural Texts", 162). To the extent that a text prompts its reader to attend to its techniques, it exerts some control over how much he experiences the literary work to be external to himself or to arise from his inner world.

of being'" ("Words and Moods", 111). The sounds of words shape us long before we learn to comprehend their meanings. By way of transitional space, literary texts are able to access that early experience of transformation through the "voice-feeling" they conduct by their form, and so they have the capacity through means beyond our awareness to influence our "grammar of being" or our patterns of experiencing the world.

This power of the form of literary language is further enhanced by literature's tendency to evoke for readers experiences which activate the full range of the senses. While all the arts involve the senses, literature, as Schwab observes, "is the one that most distinctly appeals not to one sense primarily, but — through its discursive mediation – actively engages and mobilizes all senses simultaneously" ("Cultural Texts", 172). This mediated tangibility of literary experience is what enables it to make hidden or formless self-states accessible or available — experience-able — to the self through transitional space. Wolfgang Iser, one of the founders of the Constance school of reception theory where Schwab was trained, also describes the capacity of literature to give shape to the shapeless, what he calls "ungraspables", though he is not writing from a psychoanalytic perspective. According to Iser, "literature generates the illusion of a perception, so that the inconceivable may gain presence" (212). But for Iser, the "ungraspables" that literature makes conceivable refer not to hidden psychic states or ways of being but to aspects of reality inevitably excluded from knowledge by the systems of thought necessary for sense-making. Whether the "ungraspables" are hidden aspects of the self or the exclusions in our systems of thought with which Iser is concerned, literary texts utilize our everyday techniques of perceiving and imagining to create for the reader "the illusion of a perception" that gives "the inconceivable" presence, a presence that can feel experientially as "real" as those we encounter in daily life. The density of that experience can facilitate the literary work's location in the reader's transitional space, as a tangible object — or presence — originating both from without and within. And its location in transitional space leaves the reader's self especially open to being affected or changed by that presence. When a text within transitional space gives imaginary shape to what would be otherwise ungraspable, that newly perceptible entity or state becomes accessible, becomes present to the self at a level where self-other conceptions are fluid and open to reshaping. Thus, the mobilization of the senses that literary texts accomplish is one more capacity of literature that makes it an especially effective transitional object.

A final feature that makes literary texts ideal transitional objects and potential carriers for the effect I've described is the openness of literary language to unconscious activity. That a text might communicate more or differently than its writer intended need not mean, as some recent theorists tend to claim, that language in some abstracted sense bears a level of independent agency, controlling the writer from outside her in ways of which she is not aware. The agent may instead be the writer's unconscious. A writer makes myriad choices, only a fraction of which are calculated, particularly in literary composition where the texture of language — the feel of the words — and the atmosphere of the world the text creates are as essential to the work as the meanings the words convey. Under these conditions, in Schwab's words, ". . . language may stage a performance of the unconscious and thus open up an ambivalent communicative space for what is otherwise excluded from communication" (*Subjects*, 32). The unconscious of the author, shaped in countless ways by the environment in which she lives, contributes to the shape of the text she writes, which then resonates with and influences that text's readers, and space is made through the vehicle of a literary text for the communication of what would be otherwise excluded.

Literary texts, then, function as ideal transitional objects because they are transactional in nature — between text and reader — and because the language which is their medium, through its emphasis on form that conveys voice, its evocation of sensory experience, and its openness to unconscious communication, is especially capable of recalling and reactivating in readers early experiences of self-formation. Through readers' deep and compelling emotional engagement with literary texts a central (perhaps *the* central) contribution of literature is realized. As hidden parts of the self become available for change, the stance (or mood) the text evokes leaves its imprint on the reader, affecting her way of being in the world and potentially enabling her to be more responsive to her complex and ever-changing environment. Perhaps this function of literary reading has been difficult to identify and describe because it tends to be unconscious, producing powerful experiences that can feel diminished when one attempts to put them into words. With its theorization of psychological operations beyond conscious awareness, object relations theory elucidates this valuable contribution that literary reading can make to human life and society in terms of transitional space.

Literature, Transitional Space, and Cultural Contact
The importance of the inner processing that literary texts can facilitate extends beyond the interests of the individual to affect cultures as well, as I suggested earlier. This is a central emphasis of Schwab's work on the subject, in contrast to most reader-response theorists, like Rosenblatt and Iser, who have tended to leave the issue of culture unaddressed. As Schwab observes, unless we face a thoroughly foreign text or a radically different style, we easily forget that reading "always requires a certain negotiation of otherness, a mediation between two more or less different cultural or historical contexts, the text's and the reader's" (*The Mirror*, 9). This negotiation across cultures that literary reading

necessarily involves takes on even greater import in light of the psychic location of the interaction between text and reader. Because literary reading can take up residence in the transitional space of readers where self-other or inner-outer boundaries are fluid, this form of cultural contact is capable of deeply influencing readers' experiences of difference and patterns of relating to otherness. As both a transitional object and a site for cultural contact, a literary text can potentially intervene in a reader's ways of relating shaped by her cultural location. Then as readers are affected by the texts they read so are the cultures which the readers both inhabit and to which they contribute. A literary text taken up by many individual readers can influence a culture's way of being in the world as the readers within that culture are affected, merging, in a sense, the psychological with the cultural, and establishing for literature a function of even broader significance. The reading of literary texts as transitional objects can potentially change intercultural ways of relating as well as the interpersonal and the intrapsychic, as boundaries at all these levels become open to reworking.

A couple of features of this intercultural operation that works of literature can enact are worth mentioning. First is that a literary text's influence on readers comes through its formal qualities as much or even more than through the events, experiences, and practices it conveys. As Schwab claims, it is literary form that to a large extent shapes a text's "figurations of otherness", and that because style, structure, and mood tend to operate at a subliminal level, a text's formal qualities "may, in fact, shape experiences of otherness even more deeply than [its] historical or cultural remoteness" (*The Mirror*, 43). Because a text has been given form by an author, that form — language, rhythm, perspective, tone — mediates the text's otherness for the reader, shaping the stance a reader can take toward that alternative world. In this way, what a text says may be less influential in its effect on a reader's cultural encounter than how it says it.

That a literary work has been written points to another property of this form of cultural interaction, which Schwab highlights by contrasting the cultural contact of literary reading with an anthropologist's "reading" of other cultures. The uninvited intrusion of any ethnographic reading of another culture has been considered by some to constitute a sort of violence. Texts, however, are written to be read. While reading necessarily involves some misreading, in some cases to an extent that might seem destructive or violent, a reader's interaction with a text is far from an uninvited intrusion as it is the purpose for which the text was written in the first place. Not only does this purpose lessen the potential violence in the contact between the reader's culture and the text's, but literary reading can affect other occasions of cultural contact as well. Schwab writes, "Practiced as a virtual encounter with otherness, reading may, in certain cases, precisely help to reduce the structural or cultural violence of reading the other/Other that is such a central concern in current theories" (*The Mirror*, 39). The text works to shape the way in which it is read — the way that its reader relates to the culture it embodies — and so the text itself can potentially become a sort of agent in an effort to diminish the violence of cultural contact in general. Through a measure of resonance with the reader's world, a literary text can take up residence in its reader's transitional space where his self-other boundaries are temporarily fluid, allowing the text's form to reshape his experience of Other and others and his ways of relating to them, a transformation whose repercussions extend to the culture in which he dwells.

This conception of the psychological and cultural effect of literary texts used as transitional objects is the key contribution a psychoanalytic perspective makes to the question of the function of literary reading, and it successfully brings together an understanding of the human benefit of literature (its instructiveness) with the way of reading many readers find pleasurable. When a reader gets carried away by a book, allowing her sense of the boundary between herself and the world of a literary work to blur for a time, that text becomes available to her as a valuable means of self-formation and transformation, providing relief, in Winnicott's words from "the strain of relating inner and outer reality" (13). Temporarily inhabiting an alternative world leaves its imprint on her ways of being in the world and ways of relating to others, allowing a more responsive redrawing of those self-other boundaries. Taking on the images and moods of a literary work can give form to otherwise inaccessible parts of herself, making them available for her knowing and also for change. Significantly, this conception of literary function does not depend solely on a representational role of texts — what they say about the world — and the interpretive and analytical skills required to use them in that role. Instead of benefiting the reader primarily through her understanding of what the text says about the world (and whatever use that knowledge may serve), literary works as transitional objects benefit the reader through her experience of the text, an experience of a way of being in the world, which leaves its effect not only on her understanding but, more influentially, on her own way of being in the world. Literary function, from this perspective, is not only a matter of knowledge or content but also of attitude or manner, not just what we see but how we see it, through what eyes. A strength of this conception is that it values the experience of reading which more likely drives the love of literature to which many readers attest. Intense emotional engagement with a text is not a distraction from careful analysis and critique, but is the central vehicle for obtaining a key benefit of literary reading. Though interpretation, analysis, and critique certainly serve important roles in the study of literature, the engaged experience of reading the text takes on new value from this psychoanalytic perspective. But here I'm touching on the subject of ways of reading literature, an important question in its own right, especially in light of literary texts' role as transitional objects. It is to this question that I'll turn next before returning to the issue from which this study originally arose: the teaching of literature.

2 From Words on Paper to an Object in Transitional Space: Reading for the Formative Use of Literature

As I sought to establish in the previous chapter, literary reading is valuable for individuals and for society because it functions as an especially effective occasion for re-working our conceptions of ourselves and others. Through it our way of being in the world can be altered or modified as it accesses psychological states where self-other boundaries are fluid and open to change. Literary reading's location in transitional space between inner experience and the external world makes possible this formative role, essential not only for children and youth who are still maturing but equally for adults who need the inner flexibility to adjust to a continually changing environment. What then does it take for a text to become a transitional object for a person who reads it? What does the activity of reading entail that makes a story or poem available to a reader for use in transitional space?

While my initial and ultimate interest remains in pedagogy, I must first turn to the question of reading because in and of itself this formative function of literature is insufficient as a guide or focus for instruction. Since its workings are both largely unconscious and highly individual, the use of literary texts as objects in transitional space cannot be directly taught. While an instructor can teach someone *about* this function of literature, she cannot show someone how to *do* it, to use literature in this way. Besides a conceptual understanding of the formative use of literature, what can be taught are ways of reading that might either facilitate or limit students' capacity to use texts in this way. This chapter offers an investigation into the process of reading. Though this chapter, like the last, will remain largely theoretical, it is motivated by my interest in what can transpire between student and teacher in a literature classroom, and it is informed by the experiences and insights of some exemplary teachers of literature.

The subject of reading, though, is not only of pedagogical interest. Within any theoretical approach to texts lie assumptions about how to read, a matter that may be of more significance and a better focus for argument than the more explicit concerns of the theoretical approach — the deconstructionist's emphasis on the slipperiness of language, for instance, or the historicist's interest in the context from which the work emerged. Rather than arguing about theories, in Denis Donoghue's words, it is "more worthwhile to ask adepts of feminism, Marxism, Deconstruction, the New Historicism, and Cultural Studies what they think they're doing when they read literature", because, he has concluded, ". . . theories matter only when they coerce someone's way of reading a book" (36). "Then," he adds, "they matter a lot" (36). Certainly, schools of thought like Cultural Studies and New Historicism carry significant implications for what it means to read a literary text. In fact, I might characterize my graduate education as a series of surprises at what some had thought to do with literature, ways of reading that had never occurred to me.

It is this very matter that lies at the heart of the concerns of Lentricchia, Tompkins, and Farrell, which I discussed in the introduction of this project. When Lentricchia announces he is abandoning the practice of criticism, he is rejecting the way of reading he believes it requires for the way of reading he has long loved. In undoing her own teaching practice, Tompkins is searching for a pedagogy more consistent with the way of reading she had found personally meaningful than the treatment of texts implied by her own graduate education. And, when Frank Farrell asserts that the literary criticism of recent decades makes it difficult to see why literature matters at all, it is the ways of reading underlying those critical approaches that seem to call into question literature's importance.

If the significance of different theoretical approaches to texts resides largely in their coercion of the way someone reads a book, then it is important to make those implications for reading as explicit as possible in order to be fully aware of what it is we think we are doing when we read literature, and of what that way of reading makes possible and what it excludes. Thus it becomes imperative, even beyond my pedagogical concern, to ask this question: If literature can serve a valuable psychological and social role in self-formation, what does that claim imply for how one reads a poem or novel?

Literary Reading and the Self's State in Transitional Space

The implications for how we read of this psycho-social function of literature arise from an understanding of the state of the self in transitional space. A return to Christopher Bollas' work will provide a description of that state. Whether an individual chooses the object — a poem, a musical recording, a sunset — or encounters it by chance, she must momentarily get lost in the encounter, or, perhaps more accurately, lose her awareness of her self as separate, enabling the object and her self to merge temporarily in that intermediate area between subject and object, transitional space. Getting lost in moments of experience, according to Bollas, when one "is not being . . . thoughtful", or reflective, but is "a rather simplified consciousness, even out of touch with himself for a moment", enables the subject to project meaning into the object, "to invest the object world with psychic potential" (22). This sort of investment is an unconscious action that involves abandoning "self objectification" and surrendering to the experience, "a dissolution", Bollas writes, "essential to the subjectification of reality" (53). Getting lost in the experience of an object temporarily loosens the otherwise fixed boundaries between self and other, opening those boundaries for re-working and investing the object with aspects of the self, leaving it with a powerful subjective significance.

But this loss of self-awareness or separateness is not usually a state of much duration in adulthood, because it is quickly followed by a return to the self-consciousness necessary for reflection and for normal functioning. Of these two modes, Bollas writes, "The simple experiencing self and the complex reflecting self enable the person to process life according to different yet interdependent modes of engagement: one immersive, the other reflective" (15). Each mode is important for processing lived experience, but the transitional space of self-formation requires the immersive mode — getting lost in the experience of an object which shapes us — in order for the self to re-enter momentarily that undifferentiated state of early childhood in which self and object are merged.

The act of submitting oneself to this kind of experience of an object necessarily involves some risks, both real and perceived, and therefore demands a level of confidence in the process. According to Bollas, the capacity to "devolve consciousness into the creative fragmentations of unconscious work" requires "a basic trust in the reliable relation" between such unconscious work and consciousness, trust in "the wisdom of surrender to subjectifications", helped by our knowledge that "we will awaken from our dreaming" and will return to "episodes of self observation and analysis" (53). The individual who is willing to get lost in his experience of an object, a state much like dreaming, is one who believes that he will again emerge from that state.

Not only is there the perceived risk that the self may not emerge from this sort of fusion with the object, but there is, according to Winnicott, a "precariousness" in any form of "play" as transitional experience because it "is always on the theoretical line between the subjective and that which is objectively perceived" (50). Holding in unresolved tension the paradox this-is-me and this-is-not-me requires a capacity to tolerate the instability of this tension. There is also the risk of the unknown outcome of the self's experience of an object, who we might become as we relinquish ourselves to its influence. That the transitional use of an object involves subjecting oneself to the uncertainty of the effect of transitional experience, to the unsettledness and tension of unresolved paradox, and to the threat of the apparent possibility of a permanent loss of self make this process a risky undertaking, but one that actually is reliable and, Bollas emphasizes, is the source of great joy (53). In order, then, for an individual to use an object in transitional space to give shape to her conception of self and other — her way of being in the world — she must undergo the risks of temporarily letting go of her awareness of her self and allow herself to get lost in her experience of the object, before returning to a reflective, self-conscious mode of being. Only in this state does her self-other boundaries loosen, and she becomes receptive to the influence of the object, its transformative effect.

This state or stance of the self in transitional space then has obvious implications for literary reading if a text is to serve this formative function. The reader must allow himself to become immersed in the text, to let go temporarily of a sense of himself as distinct as he surrenders himself to the experience the text provokes.[1] Of this state Gabriele Schwab explains, "Just as the author of poetic language derealizes him or herself in order to speak voices that are neither wholly I nor Not-I, so the reader, too, has to temporarily suspend his or her own boundaries during the reception process in order to slip into an imaginary world made of alien thoughts, voices, and characters" (*Subjects*, 39–40). "Derealizing" oneself, allowing one's boundaries to soften and open as one enters the world of the text and takes on the new way of being given form by the text, places the reader in the transitional space where the line between self and text blurs, and the self becomes receptive to change. Schwab refers to the "malleability" and "plasticity" of the reader's boundaries in this mode of literary reading (*Subjects*, 40). The term "permeability" comes to mind as the text takes up residence within the reader while the reader at the same time inhabits the world of the text. But along with this immersive state, the formative use of literature also involves a subsequent return to a reflective mode of engagement with the text, when the reader stands back, in a sense, and "considers where he has been" (Bollas, 31).

Making Visible the Moves of the Reader
Is this way of reading, where one immerses oneself in the world of the text, a natural or inevitable outcome of learning to read in the most general sense of the term? J. Hillis Miller assumes as much when he suggests that the ability to give oneself over to the task of recreating the world of the text within oneself "is probably more or less universal, once you have learned to read, once you have learned, that is, to turn those mute and

---

1 Like any engaging work, analysis or critique of a text can itself become a transitional activity when the reader becomes fully absorbed in it, but then the transitional "object" is not the world of the text but the reader's act of analysis. The boundary that is blurred is not between the reader as subject and the text's world as an other, but between the reader and whatever features of the text are the focus of study as well as the patterns of thought and attention involved in the analysis.

objectively meaningless shapes into letters, words, and sentences that correspond to spoken language" (118). My own experience as a reader seems to confirm Miller's speculation, but some experiences I have had as a teacher with students in community college classrooms call it into question. Before inquiring into some of the surprises I encountered with student readers, I want to examine a few of my own memories of reading for what they imply about the process of acquiring the ability to use literature as a transitional object.

My own experiences as a reader . . . and a teacher
A few years ago an experience demonstrated for me the formative power of literary reading in my own childhood. Anna, my then seven-year-old daughter, was summarizing for me a story from a picture book a teacher had read to her class. At first I recognized nothing of the story, but gradually an uncanny feeling of despair welled up in me accompanied by a sense of anticipation. As Anna's retelling continued, the small tragedy at the heart of the story was miraculously transformed into a triumph (by the provision of magic golden winged shoes, of course), and I was amazed to feel a powerful but somehow anticipated surprise that approached awe as my sense of despair was relieved. I knew I had read that story before because of how deeply my daughter's simple retelling of it affected me. That sense was confirmed later when her teacher let me look at the picture book itself, and I found some of its images familiar. Yet I have no memory of reading the book as a child or having it read to me, no memory of ever having seen it among the shelves of books in my childhood home. All I can recall, apart from a few familiar images restored for me by looking again at the book, was this pervasive state of despair followed by an unexpected relief. The strength of the feeling state produced in me by a mere retelling of the story seems to indicate that in encountering this book as a young child, probably in having it read to me not more than a few times, I had experienced it as an object in transitional space. It had become invested with psychic significance as it evoked for me an experience of despair transformed into joy. It seems that I already had the capacity to use a text as a transitional object in some of my earliest encounters with books.

Once I was able to read myself, as I now recall, I regularly used literary texts as sources of a sort of satisfaction, a way to meet what felt like an undefined emotional need. I can remember as a nine- or ten-year-old often standing before our small closet full of children's books at home, looking for just the right book to fit my mood. And then I remember the delight and gratification of those times that I succeeded at finding one that felt "right", reading it, and having just the experience I had a "taste" for. By junior high I'd become a voracious reader as I came to prefer the time I spent in the worlds of The Chronicles of Narnia and The Lord of the Rings to my own real world, colored as it was in those years by some painful turmoil in my family. The influence on me of some of those books has become apparent as I've returned to them in adulthood to read them aloud to my own children and found myself at times moved to tears as I re-experience parts of their worlds that still feel deeply resonant. But not all books I encountered in adolescence offered worlds I welcomed. I quickly regretted reading one about a number of youth trapped in some sort of behaviorist experiment because of the sense of bleakness it left behind in me. And I put down *The Lord of the Flies* after finding the boys' increasing cruelty to be an unbearable experience for me. (I've never picked it up since.)

During my college years, the nature of the reading experiences I found deeply significant shifted somewhat. The literary works I found most moving — Eliot's *Four Quartets*, Morrison's *Song of Solomon*, and Mann's *Doctor Faustus*, for instance — were those on which I wrote papers for classes, and their significance to me only emerged after I'd initially read them and then had gone back through them to work out something about them that had interested me as a focus for a class paper. It seems that I was able to translate texts like these into experiences capable of serving as objects in transitional space only with considerable probing and thought, but with that effort or perhaps in the process of exerting that effort they yielded experiences of such depth that I still feel a powerful emotional connection to those texts.

Because this formative use of objects is largely an unconscious process, it is difficult to determine when it has taken place. The indications I'm using — the signs that point to likely transitional activity — are a deep emotional sense that a text has impacted or affected me and the return of a pervasive feeling state when I recall a particular text, though those feeling states or senses of effect may be negative (say, repulsion) as well as positive. As my reflections on my own reading experiences indicate, it indeed seems that I was able to translate verbal text into a transitional object even before I was able to read the words on the page myself. It is a skill I can not remember ever needing to learn, but seemed to be automatic or inevitable, or perhaps, to use Miller's word, "universal". And I managed to keep hold of that reading practice even in the midst of taking on the intellectual, reflective activity of composing college-student literary criticism. It was with some surprise, then, that I discovered that many of the students in my community college classrooms did not share my ability to have a meaningful experience with some fairly simple texts that I'd found engaging.

Though I was teaching in a composition program where literary reading was not an emphasis, I did use some short literary texts as focal points for reflection and writing. In one of the very first composition courses I taught, I assigned a piece of Mark Twain's satire that I'd found provocative and delightful, fully expecting that my students would respond similarly. What I heard instead, first from one outspoken student and then from most of the others in the class, was that they could make nothing of the text at all. They were mystified by it. Though I repeatedly adjusted my expectations of students' reading capabilities, I still met responses I didn't expect. Another that truly surprised me occurred in one of the more recent courses I taught. A couple of students, outspoken ones again, claimed to have found Flannery O'Connor's "Everything that Rises Must Converge" to be a waste of time. In the class discussion that followed these pronouncements, no one admitted to finding the story, which I have always found deeply moving, to be anything more than strange, perplexing, or boring.[2] It is this kind of student response that seems to have led one literature instructor, Daniel Green, to conclude that most students have no need for literature since they show such little interest in it, as he contended in an editorial in *College English* (285). But instead of resigning myself to the inevitability of their indifference, I want to ask what is it that I do as a reader that these students can't or don't do. What is going on that makes our experiences of texts so different?

Undoubtedly certain skills and a greater familiarity with some kinds of texts would have helped my students in their reading of Mark Twain and Flannery O'Connor. Some exposure to satire and some assistance with Twain's highly stylized, archaic language in this particular piece of writing may have enabled them to make more of his text. And in my later class, it appeared in our discussion that none of the students were able to pick up O'Connor's sharp irony, leaving her short story seemingly pointless or at least puzzling to them. Much has been written about the skills and background knowledge necessary to make meaning from literary texts, particularly those that are especially complex. In her book on teaching literature, Elaine Showalter offers a list of competencies that she claims should be the aim of a literary education. Her list includes, "How to read figurative language and distinguish between literal and metaphorical meaning", "How to detect the cultural assumptions underlying writings from a different time or society, and in the process to become aware of one's own cultural assumptions", and "How to relate apparently disparate works to one another, and to synthesize ideas that connect them into a tradition or a literary period" (27). Sheridan Blau takes a different approach to competencies in his book on literary pedagogy, providing instead a list of traits or attitudes displayed

---

2 There were a few texts that a high percentage of my students over the years seemed to find meaningful or moving. The one to which I received a fairly consistent enthusiastic response was a prize-winning student essay about her relationship with her brother in their adolescence, a subject and a level of writing sophistication which my students seemed to find accessible.

by those able to, in his words, "perform as autonomous, engaged readers of difficult literary texts" (210). Traits he lists include, a "capacity for sustained, focused attention", a "willingness to suspend closure", and a "tolerance for ambiguity, paradox, and uncertainty" (211). But, while these skills or traits are certainly valuable, is literary reading essentially a matter of distinguishing between literal and metaphorical meaning and relating disparate works to one another, or maintaining focused attention and suspending closure?

When a process of any kind appears to occur naturally or without effort, as meaningful encounters with texts have occurred for me and, likely, for most other teachers and many students of literature, that process can easily remain invisible. We've had no reason or opportunity to notice what it is we're doing when we can do it without apparent effort. The essentials of the process may best become visible when the process itself fails — when what we expect to take place effortlessly between reader and book does not occur. Showalter's list of competencies and Blau's list of traits may indicate the areas of failure they've observed in their students, skills or attributes their students lacked which prevented them from fully interacting with literary texts in the ways their instructors expected. But in both Showalter's and Blau's formulations the heart of literary reading — the fundamental moves that make it possible for a reader to have a meaningful experience of a text — are still assumed or taken for granted and so remain hidden. To make visible what literary reading essentially involves requires an examination of the failure of the reading process at a much more fundamental level, a level of reading failure unlikely to appear in a college classroom. It is this fundamental failure of the reading process that is the focus of one middle-school teacher and teacher educator's research. Jeffrey Wilhelm's investigation into the practices of his seventh- and eighth-grade remedial reading students, students who actively resisted reading of any kind, makes visible the moves that are essential to literary reading, the process capable of translating words on paper into experiences available as objects in transitional space.[3] Though most students who arrive in a college literature course will likely already be adept at the most basic moves of literary reading with which Wilhelm's students struggle, Wilhelm's project is of value for college-level teachers because it brings these fundamentals to conscious awareness enabling an instructor at any level to ensure that they are fostered in a course and not overlooked. For this reason Wilhelm's research is worth examination as part of my project.

---

3 In my discussion of Wilhelm's study of middle school readers, it will become apparent that I am not concerned about distinguishing between fictional texts that might be considered more or less *literary*, but am interested in literary reading in the broadest sense of the term.

Jeffrey Wilhelm's remedial readers

As may be a common practice of teachers at all levels, Wilhelm acknowledges that in his early years of teaching he likely derived his sense of success only from his most enthusiastic students (1–2). Each year he encountered a few students who resisted reading, but he admits that he just gave up on them ever becoming readers and focused his efforts on those who were more responsive. It was when he was asked to teach the remedial reading class and encountered a whole classroom of resistant readers that he could no longer blame them for their resistance (7). Instead he sought to do everything he could to help them overcome it. But, as he writes, "Despite free reading and reading workshops, journals, literary letter exchanges, and a variety of response activities, many of my students did not seem to improve as readers, and many more continued to resist reading", leading him to conclude that "for most of my student readers, engagement with literature through the aesthetic stance [in Rosenblatt's formulation] did not occur naturally or spontaneously" (22). Some essential practice or skill was missing in those students' reading process that prevented engagement with a text from occurring. It is from this position that Wilhelm begins his inquiry, seeking to discover what it is that his resistant students did not do in their reading that students of his who were avid readers did. His investigation into his students' reading practices took the form of think-aloud protocols (where students describe the mental activities they perceive themselves doing as they are reading a text), attitudinal inventories, reading logs, and interviews, conducted to a limited extent among all of his students during one academic year, but also focused in much greater depth on a number of selected students, both some he identified as avid readers and some resistant readers.

Through extensive interviews and think-aloud protocols with three avid readers from his classes — students who enjoyed reading and read much both in and out of school — Wilhelm sought to establish what those readers did as they read. From this inquiry he identified ten "dimensions of response" to a literary text, mental activities these readers regularly practiced in reading (46). These ten are: *entering the story world, showing interest in the story, relating to characters,* and *seeing the story world,* comprising the evocative category of dimensions; *elaborating on the story world* and *connecting literature to life,* comprising the connective category of dimensions; and *considering significance, recognizing literary conventions, recognizing reading as a transaction,* and *evaluating an author and the self as reader,* comprising the reflective category of dimensions (46–47). Though Wilhelm identifies three categories of reader response, I find Wilhelm's middle category, the connective, to be unnecessary in that *elaborating on the story world* serves to assist the reader in evoking a world from the text while *connecting literature to life* can be considered a reflective activity.[4] I would instead consider these activities to fall into two categories: those that assist the reader in entering the world of the text and those that involve standing back from the text to reflect on it, general moves in reading that notably resemble Bollas' identification of the immersive and the reflective stages of a self's transitional use of an object.

What I found striking as I read Wilhelm's description of these reading moves is how clearly they are evident in comments his avid student readers make about their reading. One of these students, a young man whose reading of fiction like Tom Clancy's often gets in the way of his school work, offers an unforgettable description of the process of immersing oneself in the world of the text. Wilhelm quotes this student,

> When you're not into a book yet, it's really obvious [laughs]. It's like you're standing in line for the diving board on a windy day and you're freezing your nuts off. If you'll excuse the expression [laughs]. Where was I? Oh yeah. It's like you're in pain and you have your arms wrapped around you and the concrete is scratching your feet. The first part of the story is the line and the ladder and the board. When everything comes together and you jump it's like you're in this underwater world like INSTANTLY and then you just stay down there and never come up until someone makes you.
>
> (55 bracketed notes Wilhelm's)

For this reader, engaging with a work of fiction feels so much like immersing himself in another world that he compares it to jumping off a diving board into a swimming pool and staying underwater, reluctant to come up. Entrance into that world is for him as all-consuming as the experience of being underwater. So eager or impatient is he to enter the alternative world of the text that he experiences the anticipation as a sort of pain.

While this student vividly articulates the experience of immersing oneself in a text, the comment of another student captures a sense of the apparent effortlessness of this immersive mode of literary reading. In the midst of describing the scene she sees in her imagination as she recreates the world of the text she is reading, she interrupts herself to observe: "It's almost like I've stopped reading and I'm dreaming, I guess . . ." (68). Her choice of the word "dreaming" to describe the effortlessness of this

---

4 In a forthcoming book, *Teaching Literacy for Love and Wisdom: "Being the Book" and "Being the Change"* (Teachers College Press), Jeffrey Wilhelm and Bruce Novak make a fascinating and convincing case for the connective dimension of reading consisting this time of the reader's sense of connection with an implied author from whom the reader receives the text as a sort of gift. In this view reading becomes a key facilitator of human community.

readerly state echoes Bollas' comparison of the transitional use of objects to a sort of dreaming, "the dream work of one's life" (53).

For these highly engaged readers, the reflective mode of reading appears to be no less automatic or "natural" than the immersive mode, often seeming to arise spontaneously from their experience of the text. The close interaction between the two modes is evident in a couple of comments these students make about their reading. The student for whom reading is like jumping off a diving board observes, "Sometimes I'll be reading and something will just knock my socks off and I'll say, 'Whoa! How'd he [the author] do that to me?' I mean, how did he shock me like that or make me feel that way?" (75, bracketed note Wilhelm's). Though this reader claims that he emerges from his underwater alternative world only when "someone makes" him, this remark shows that his experience of the text itself can prompt him to step back enough to reflect on how the text is able to affect him. The comment of another student demonstrates two different levels of critical reflection prompted by her reading of a text. She says, "I was really surprised by the ending and . . . I think, 'What did the author do to make me expect another ending?' Then I'll ask if there was a point to the twist or if it's just to surprise me" (76). Her surprise provokes her to ask how the author produced the effect and then to wonder why, for what end.

Though the objective of Wilhelm's inquiry into the reading practices of student readers was to elicit or illuminate these readerly moves, his investigation also disclosed another aspect of students' reading experience that is of value for my study. The comments and the habits of those of Wilhelm's students who claim to enjoy reading revealed that they considered the reading they enjoy to have no place at school. Wilhelm observes, ". . . the reading they valued was pursued in study halls, at home, with friends and family — usually anyplace but the classroom" (26). In general his students did not expect school reading "to be fun, engaging, or personally satisfying" (26). One of these students told Wilhelm that in school "reading is being able to answer the questions at the end of a story", while many others agreed that reading in school meant "answering questions" or "finding answers", including one of the avid student readers Wilhelm interviewed who claimed that this sort of "'snipe hunting' . . . was what 'makes me hate reading for school'" (9–10). For Wilhelm's middle school readers the reading activities generally asked of them at school, with their apparent emphasis on right answers, seemed more to thwart their engaged reading than to encourage or develop it.

A need to develop the ability to engage with texts is far more evident in the resistant student readers who are the focus of the rest of Wilhelm's study, students who not only demonstrated extremely low reading ability but who seemed actively to avoid reading of any kind both in and out of class. What Wilhelm found missing in the reading practices of the weaker readers in his classes was a move essential to the ability to immerse themselves in the imaginary world of the text. In the first twelve weeks of the study, Wilhelm observes, many of the less proficient readers and all those identified as learning disabled "failed to reveal a single move on the dimension of visualizing or seeing what they read," leading him to conclude that these students "seemed to be entirely unable to visualize a secondary world without some sort of artistic aid . . ." (65). Many of these students also "expressed incredulity" when asked questions "about what they were 'seeing' or when other students described what they saw while reading" (65). Not only does Wilhelm's study indicate that the weaker readers in his classes did not "see" what they read, but that without such visualization they were unable to make any of the other readerly moves that his engaged student readers demonstrated (65). From these findings he concludes that teachers "often ask less engaged readers to reflect on something that they have not experienced" (88). Everything else that one might do with a literary text seems to depend upon first evoking from it an experience.

Remarkably, Wilhelm notes, students at his school who were not able to perform the reading activities asked of them tended to be put into a supplemental reading program that focused solely on phonics and word recognition, considered in the program to be the foundation of learning to read. Wilhelm found that many of his learning-disabled students who had been through this program displayed very negative and resistant attitudes toward reading (12). If reading depends upon an ability to create a world from a text, one might expect that reducing the process to a matter of letter-sound correspondence and word recognition would only further frustrate students already mystified by the challenge of making meaning from a text. The practices of the struggling readers in Wilhelm's classes made evident that these students conceived of reading merely as decoding or sounding out words, matching the emphasis of the instruction they'd received.

In response to these findings, Wilhelm uses his time in class with these less proficient readers to attempt to help them develop an experience of the texts they read through drama and art. By having students act out portions of a text either by playing the characters themselves or by using cut-outs they make of a text's characters, including one for themselves as the reader, Wilhelm found ways, as he says, ". . . of bringing the invisible secrets of engaged readers out into the open, where they could be observed and shared and tried on by other readers" (85). The effect was significant of making visible for less-engaged and resistant readers the world-making process of reading, and many of these students became enthusiastic readers. One of these students, one who had regularly announced to Wilhelm, "Reading is stupid", upon entering his remedial reading classroom (11), was so helped by the drama activities that he subsequently spent the entirety of three study periods reading a book by his own choice. When he'd finished it, he announced to a teacher that this "is the first book I ever read by myself", and then added, "I liked it, and I don't want anybody to ask me any questions about it" (110), as if to keep the typical school practice of question and answer from ruining the experience he felt so good about. Another once-resistant, now eager reader expressed what he had learned from his class's story dramas with these words: "You have to live the story . . . You have to be the book" (110). In its sense of merging the self and the text, his description of the act of reading, as he had come to understand it from acting out portions of the text, is striking for its correspondence to the concept of transitional space.

Students' use of paper cutouts of characters and other significant objects from a story to act out what they read also produces clear evidence of a transitional use of texts, as it allows them to position themselves as readers within their re-enactment. The relationship between self and story emerges most clearly in a student's retelling of a story, in this instance one passed on orally rather than in writing. This struggling reader in a class of Wilhelm's, a usually taciturn English language learner and Hmong refugee, used cutouts of characters that she had drawn to tell the class a Hmong tale, which had been passed down in her family. According to Wilhelm, her performance of the story of a princess cursed by an evil crow was elaborate and almost twenty-five minutes in length, and "held her listeners enthralled" (129). What I found most interesting in Wilhelm's account of her performance was his description of her use of a cutout of herself to make visible her own position in the story as she retold it. Wilhelm writes,

> During the princess's great troubles under the curse, she placed the princess cutout over the cutout of herself as reader and said, "I cared about princess the most. She did nothing wrong. Why do they want to burn her up and stuff? I feel like I her and I feel very sad. She not understand why everyone so mean to her." She then placed the reader cutout over that of the crow and said, "I hate him. He evil. I want to cover him up." At the end of the story she again overlaid the princess cutout on her own, and said, "I am like princess the most. I love her the most. I want to be strong like her."
>
> (130)

With these paper cutouts, some of which she redrew several times until she thought they really "look and feel like people in the story" (130), this student was able to tangibly represent her immersion in the story world, her powerful identification with one of the characters of the story and her equally powerful identification against another, giving her audience and us a sort of glimpse into her use of transitional space. A colleague of

Wilhelm's rightly identified this story representation activity as, "as sweet a piece of metacognition as you can imagine", through which students "can actually be let into [others'] heads and see what others see when they read" (142).

For this student and for a couple of others, drawing also served a more foundational role in their reading process than that of making visible their world-making activity for others. Their ability to engage with a text at all required frequent opportunities to stop reading and draw out characters and scenes for themselves. Their own illustrations were necessary to enable them to visualize what they read, and then reading became for them a meaningful activity.

Though these formerly resistant readers' interactions with texts did not achieve in their year in Wilhelm's class the depth and complexity of those of the highly engaged readers, these students did exhibit a new and vital level of engagement with texts and enthusiasm for reading. The key to their transformation was the opportunity to "see" the world-making task of literary reading in action and to be pushed to undertake the same imaginative activity themselves. The tangible aids of drama and art supported their own attempts to create the world of the story in their imaginations. Their accounts of that process use terms that indicate a merging of self and text, a permeability of self-other boundaries as in transitional space, suggesting that what is necessary for words on paper to become available as an object in transitional space is that the reader construct from the words a world in his imagination, a world in which he can immerse himself.

Though this conclusion may seem too obvious to warrant mention, Wilhelm's study puts forward two crucial insights for any investigation into literary pedagogy: first, that the ability to recreate the alternative world of the text within oneself and to enter into that world is not universal among readers, as J. Hillis Miller assumes, but for some must be learned or prompted;[5] and, second, that this ability is the basis of all literary reading — that it makes possible the formative use of literature and that from it emerges reflection on the text and on the reader's experience of it that involve distancing oneself from the text. Wilhelm's study also makes evident how schools' treatment of literary texts can potentially undermine this process by neglecting the role of imaginative

---

5 Wilhelm's evidence does not rule out the possibility that his resistant readers might have been fully able to enter into an imaginary world through a text that included images, like a comic book or graphic novel, or through a dramatic presentation like a play or movie. One could also explore these students' experiences of being read to as young children to determine if the disconnect between hearing words and visualizing a world occurred for them with the process of learning to read in school or if the two had never been connected for them.

world-making in reading, leaving some students oblivious to its role and others convinced that it has no place in school.

Does the neglect of the role of world-making in reading evident in Wilhelm's study also affect post-secondary literature instruction? There is little research available to answer that question. In the next chapter of this project I will examine the ways that literary education is described in recent pedagogical texts as a means of ascertaining at least how the teaching of literature is conceptualized and discussed at the post-secondary level in light of these insights. But first I want to probe further into the relationship between the two broad moves or modes of literary reading so evident in Wilhelm's avid student readers: the immersive mode — the process of constructing an imaginary world from the text and immersing oneself in it, and the reflective mode — the process of stepping back from the text in order to reflect on some aspect of it.

Immersion and Reflection: The Two Moves of the Reading Process in Conflict

According to their description of their reading activity, Wilhelm's avid student readers seem to shift seamlessly or effortlessly between immersing themselves in a text and stepping back to question the text, moves that match Bollas's account of the final stages of a self's transitional use of an object. Yet this sort of easy positional movement in reading seems to be squelched in these students' experiences of instructional activities or expectations in school, as reading there becomes, in their assessment, only a means of answering questions correctly. That a difficulty in the ease of movement between these two reading modes remains (or reemerges) at more advanced levels of literary study is implied in the work of a number of literary scholars who address these modes, scholars who speak from both different decades and in some cases strikingly different schools of thought. I want to examine their treatment of these reading moves in order to identify potential challenges to the formative use of literature with which a literary pedagogy must be concerned.

The role of immersive reading

To return briefly to Gabriele Schwab's perspective, and the psychoanalytic theory that informs it, she claims that literary reading involves "derealizing" oneself as one "slips into an imaginary world" (*Subjects*, 39–40). This process of temporarily letting go of one's sense of self in order to become immersed in a new world (and in a new way of being), allowing self and text to merge for a time, releases the self-formational capabilities of literary reading, and, as Wilhelm's students have made evident, requires the imaginative activity of recreating the world of the text within oneself. A number of other literary scholars, writing from outside psychoanalytic theory, also emphasize the importance of the immersive mode of reading.

I will gather some of these statements here in order to add their insights to Schwab's and Wilhelm's.

Philip Davis's account of the power of literary reading is of interest as an illustration of an attempt to articulate the phenomena of transitional space without the language or concepts of object relations theory. Davis locates literature's power in the blurring of the boundaries between self and text, or between life and literature, but conceives of it in terms of a needed sort of category-mistake. He writes,

> I believe in all sorts of category-mistakes — confusing books with realities, thinking there is something behind the words, identifying inside with fictional characters. Category-mistakes are the places where the real power of metaphor and imagination begins, before you ever realize that this *is* metaphor, this *is* imagination. When the ignorant audience member stands up and shouts at Othello, in protest at the imminent murder of Desdemona, it may be, to put it mildly, a misplaced instinct — a misunderstanding of the nature of art and a failure of correct psychic distance. But it is the *right* thing, albeit in the wrong place.
>
> ("Place", 150)

For Davis, it is in making a category-mistake, in believing temporarily that the worlds texts create are real, that a reader allows literature to have power in life, to have an effect. On another occasion, Davis articulates this blurring of boundaries in terms of the self, and comes even close to describing transitional space. The kind of reading with which he is concerned he explains as "taking books personally to such a depth inside that you no longer have a merely secure idea of self and relevance to self, but a deeper exploratory sense of a reality somehow finding unexpected relations and echoes in you" (*Experience*, xvi). Although Davis' claims lack the conceptual grounding that object relations theory might provide, their resonance with the concept of transitional space offers additional evidence of the transitional nature of literary reading. Davis also reminds us of the role of belief in the immersive mode of literary reading — belief that the world of the text is, for the moment, real.

While Davis considers some blurring of the boundary between text and reader to be necessary for a work of literature to have any power (or value) in life, it is Louise Rosenblatt who demonstrates that the very process of reading demands much interplay between the world of the text and the world of the reader, warranting another return in this project to her conception of reading as a transaction between reader and text. To examine the activity of the reader in the process of reading, Rosenblatt distinguishes between the "text" as "a set or series of signs interpretable as linguistic symbols" and what she calls the "poem" which is the reader's experience of the text as she constructs meaning from the set of signs and, therefore, is "an event in time" and not "an object or ideal entity" (*Reader*, 12). Rosenblatt describes what takes place for a "poem" to "happen" as "a coming-together, a compenetration, of a reader and a text" (*Reader*, 12). She explains, "Under the magnetism of the ordered symbols of the text, [the reader] marshals his resources and crystallizes out from the stuff of memory, thought, and feeling a new order, a new experience, which he sees as the poem" (*Reader*, 12). The very act of reading itself, then, can be considered a sort of merging of the reader's self and the text, a "compenetration", as the reader must necessarily draw from her own memories, thoughts, and feelings to supply meaning to the linguistic symbols of the text. When I read of a wood, I initially picture a wood much like the one behind my childhood home, which brings with it a powerful feeling state of curiosity, adventure, beauty, and stillness, but I must then quickly allow the text to further shape and direct the mental image I develop of its wood and the feeling state it conveys, perhaps one of threat and foreboding. The text's wood then becomes for me a new experience of a wood, and, according to Rosenblatt, "becomes part of the ongoing stream of [my] life experience" (*Reader*, 12), adding to my real-life experiences of the wood in the backyard of my childhood.[6] If there is no resonance or correlation between the world of the text and the world of the reader, there is no meaning for the reader; the reader can make nothing of the text. When some correlation does exist, the reader must first allow the text to trigger or activate her own memories, thoughts, and feelings, and then she must allow the text to shape that which it has drawn forth into a new experience.

The making of meaning in the act of reading involves then a necessary transaction, to use Rosenblatt's term, between the reader and the text, in which the worlds of each give shape to the other, but this transaction for the reader is less calculated and methodical than it is temporarily all-consuming. Rosenblatt compares the stance or state to which the reader should aspire in this transaction to "the condition of music . . . a complete absorption in the process of evoking a work from the text, and in sensing, clarifying, structuring, savoring, that experience as it

---

6 One of Wilhelm's students offers an account of her process of visualizing the details of a text that fits perfectly with Rosenblatt's claim:

> When I read a book that takes place in a house, and it isn't really described in great detail, then I always see the same house in my mind. The house is a mixture of all of the houses I've been in. but if there are details that don't fit my idea of a house then I have to change the house. Once I do, it stays changed for the story. If too many things are different, I have to imagine a completely new house, but I'm sure that's based on what houses I've seen in my life, too.

(62–63)

unfolds" (*Reader*, 29). The literary transaction, then, is largely an immersive mode of engagement, as Rosenblatt urges the reader to become fully absorbed in the experience of the "poem" as he evokes it from the text, attending to the experience itself just as one might attend to an experience of a symphony or a rock concert. Central to such absorption or immersion in an experience is a loss or diminishment of self-consciousness as the self becomes preoccupied with the unfolding experience of the object, in this case, the literary work.

Davis and Rosenblatt each emphasize a vital role for the self in the act of reading. For Davis the reader is the location for the impact or effect of the text as she allows the world of the text to cross into her own life. For Rosenblatt the reader produces, in response to the text, the memories, thoughts, and feelings — the raw materials, so to speak — that initially supply meaning for her to the words of the text, transforming it from a series of signs into a literary experience. But both Davis and Rosenblatt also imply a moving aside of the self before the text, a sort of submission. A work of literature has power, for Davis, as the reader allows the world of the text to become, to some extent, real, an act of assent. In Rosenblatt the reader sets herself aside in two ways: as she lets the text shape the feelings and images its words evoke from her (as I permit the pleasant wood of my childhood memories to be transformed into the threatening wood of the world of the text, for instance), and also as she allows herself to let go of her self-awareness in order to become fully absorbed in her experience of the literary work. While this sort of self-derealization, to borrow Schwab's term, receives less emphasis in Davis's and Rosenblatt's formulations, it forms the heart of the reflections on reading of two others, theorists separated not only by a generation but by their widely divergent theoretical approaches: C. S. Lewis and J. Hillis Miller.

For Lewis reading is less a transaction between the self and the text than it is a laying aside of oneself and surrendering to the text. Lewis introduces this conception of literary reading by drawing an extended analogy to the viewing of paintings.

> We must not let loose our own subjectivity upon the pictures and make them its vehicles. We must begin by laying aside as completely as we can all our own preconceptions, interests, and associations. We must make room for Botticelli's Mars and Venus, or Cimabue's Crucifixion, by emptying out our own. After the negative effort, the positive. We must use our eyes. We must look, and go on looking till we have certainly seen exactly what is there. We sit down before the picture in order to have something done to us, not that we may do things with it. The first demand any work of any art makes upon us is surrender. Look. Listen. Receive. Get yourself out of the way.
>
> (18–19)

Though it is impossible to completely lay aside the preconceptions and interests one brings to a text or to any object, nor would one be able to construct any meaning from a work of art without the experiences one brings to one's encounter with the object, as Rosenblatt has convincingly demonstrated, yet Lewis's point here bears a striking resemblance to Schwab's emphasis on the "derealization" of the self in literary reading and to Bollas' claim that we submit ourselves to the transitional experience of an object, rather than imposing our own view on the "object world". For Lewis, we are to approach any work of art by getting ourselves out of the way and surrendering to the work. Lewis' apparent disagreement with Rosenblatt may not be one of opposition as much as a difference in emphasis. He does not overlook the reader entirely nor construe his role as merely passive, but asserts for the reader an "imaginative activity" which he characterizes as an "obedient one," appearing passive at first because the reader or spectator "is making sure of his orders" (20). While Rosenblatt would seem to emphasize my provision of my memory of a wood as I construct meaning from the word "wood" in the text, Lewis would stress the importance of my willingness to abandon the pleasurable connotations of that memory in the face of the foreboding feel of the wood I meet in the text.

The concept of obedience may be an unpopular one in recent years, colored by its connotations of subjection or domination. But for Lewis an act of obedience must precede any evaluation or judgment of a work of art. If, as Lewis claims, "we can judge any sentence . . . only by the work it does or fails to do", then "the effect must precede the judgment on the effect" (92). What applies to the sentence applies also to the entire work of art. "Ideally," Lewis continues, "we must receive it first and then evaluate it. Otherwise, we have nothing to evaluate" (92). Or, as he puts it in another instance, "There is no good asking first whether the work before you deserves such a surrender, for until you have surrendered you cannot possibly find out" (19). If a reader is unwilling to "obey" a text, submitting herself to its direction, she will not allow it to have an effect on her — she will not undergo an experience in transaction with the text — and therefore will be unable to "know" the text as a "poem" or work of art, in Rosenblatt's sense of the term, in order to evaluate it as such.[7]

---

7 In some cases, certain readers submitting themselves to certain texts can be traumatizing, and those readers would be wise in resisting such texts. Wayne Booth's discussion in *The Company We Keep* of his colleague's resistance to reading and teaching *The Adventures of Huckleberry Finn* is one memorable instance of this situation. While I will speak briefly to this concern later in this chapter, the potential of literary reading for producing harm rather than benefit is an important topic I hope to explore more fully in a future project.

Further developing his conception of what it means to surrender to a work of art, Lewis distinguishes between "receiving" a text and "using" it.[8]

> A work of (whatever) art can be either 'received' or 'used'. When we 'receive' it we exert our senses and imagination and various other powers according to a pattern invented by the artist. When we 'use' it we treat it as assistance for our own activities. The one, to use an old-fashioned image, is like being taken for a bicycle ride by a man who may know roads we have never yet explored. The other is like adding one of those little motor attachments to our own bicycle and then going for one of our familiar rides.
>
> (88)

Not only is the activity of the reader/spectator evident here, as we "exert our senses and imagination and various other powers", but some of the risk that Bollas and Winnicott identify with transitional space emerges in this statement as well. According to Lewis, "receiving" a work of art means following a "pattern" invented by another and being taken to places we have never been. We don't know where we might end up — or who we might be when we arrive. What does the "recipient" want with the work of art? Lewis says he "wants to rest in it", as it is for him, "at least temporarily, an end" (89). "Resting" in an object may consciously seem to be an end in itself, but, with the insights of object relations theory, it does indeed serve a sort of deeper function, though usually an unconscious one, as the object can then become available for self-formational use in transitional space, and we allow it to take us to unknown places within ourselves.

This active submission on the part of the reader before the text is also an emphasis in J. Hillis Miller's book *On Literature*. Like Lewis, Miller is concerned with allowing literary texts to have their full effect, giving them opportunity to accomplish what they are capable of producing within the reader. Miller sees the demand literary texts place on their readers captured in the command with which Melville opens *Moby Dick*, a use of language which Miller considers performative, in terms of speech act theory, because it makes something happen by way of its readers. For a literary text to make something happen in its readers, the readers must

---

8   There is an important difference between the word *use* in Lewis' context and in Bollas'. Lewis is critical of the tendency to use literary texts consciously as means to support one's own projects or interests, and so skewing one's perception or reception of the text. Bollas, on the other hand, is interested in making the objects one encounters, such as literary texts, available for an unconscious psychic use, a form of use that depends upon allowing the object to maintain an integrity of its own.

respond to the text with an act of assent. Here is Miller's account of a text's demand and the reader's response.

> The imaginary realm opened by a literary work is not simply "made available" to the reader, however. The performative dimension of the work's words demands a response from the reader. Right reading is an active engagement. It requires a tacit decision to commit all one's powers to bringing the work into existence as an imaginary space within oneself. The reader must utter, in response to the work's invocation, another performative speech act: "I promise to believe in you." . . . Tacitly uttering the first responsive performative is the formal acceptance of a contract. This saying "Yes" is the "Open Sesame!" that gives the reader access to all the rest of Melville's huge work. If you agree to call the narrator Ishmael, you can enter the work. Otherwise not. Some such response to a demand that the reader accept the particular rules of a given work is necessary to all acts of reading.
> (38–39)

This act of assent that a text demands of its readers and the accompanying effort to bring the work to life within the reader are required in order for the reader to gain access to the literary work.

Such access is key for Miller because of his conception of the unique contribution of a literary text. He argues that each literary work "opens up a singular world, attainable in no other way than by reading that work" (118). Reading, then, is the sole means by which one can enter that alternative world, and so the activity of reading becomes, for Miller, "a matter of giving one's whole mind, heart, feelings, and imagination, without reservation, to recreating that world within oneself, on the basis of the words" (118). He characterizes this readerly stance as "an innocent, childlike abandonment to the act of reading, without suspicion, reservation, or interrogation" (119). In a statement reminiscent of Lewis' claim about surrendering to a text, Miller cautions that, if this effort "is not successful, it is not even possible to know what might be dangerous about submission to the magic power of the words on the page" (119).

Why is entrance into the new worlds created by literary texts of such importance according to Miller? As I discussed in an earlier chapter, Miller simply contends, "Human beings not only have a propensity to dwell in imaginary worlds. They have a positive need to do so" (81). While Miller contributes to this investigation some insights about the activity of reading literary texts, psychoanalytic theory can fill out Miller's conception of the value of dwelling in the imaginary worlds of literature. The human need Miller identifies for entering other worlds with imaginative abandonment can be understood as the human need for self-formational activity, opportunities for re-forming one's conception of self and world through allowing one's self to merge for a time with an object in transitional space.

Just as Bollas speaks of a sort of self-abandonment and immersion in the transformational use of objects in transitional space and as Schwab refers to the "derealization" of the self in literary reading, so these others writing from outside psychoanalytic theory point to a similar letting-go of self-preoccupation in reading literature. For Davis it involves a destabilizing of the conception of self and relevance to self by a temporary merging of the text's world and the reader's. For Rosenblatt it is a "compenetration" of reader and text in their transaction, and complete absorption in the process. For Lewis literary reading means setting oneself aside and surrendering to the text. And for Miller it is a matter of assent and of fully committing all one's faculties to recreating the text's world in oneself, without reservation. Much like Wilhelm discovered in his experience with middle school remedial readers, these literary theorists recognize that a text is not fully available to a reader without such imaginative acts of abandon. But, with the insights of Bollas and Schwab, we can identify this immersive readerly stance as what makes the text available to the reader for a specific (though unconscious) purpose — the formative use of an object in transitional space.

Each seems to acknowledge that immersing oneself in reading a literary work involves, in some way, the laying aside of one's self or sense of self to enter an alternative world. But it is Miller who points out a particular difficulty of such an act for those who are "no longer children, or childlike . . . .. This is the attempt, an attempt that may well not succeed, to suspend ingrained habits of 'critical' or suspicious reading" (119). "Suspicious" reading, keeping oneself at a distance from a text, prevents a reader's immersion in a literary world and therefore can threaten the formative use of literature, a conflict that requires some focused attention.

When reflective reading undermines immersive reading
While Wilhelm's avid readers demonstrate an apparently effortless oscillation between immersing themselves in a text and stepping back to reflect on or question that text, the writings of a number of prominent literary theorists suggest that the relationship between these two broad modes of reading can be an uneasy one, especially in the context of academic literary study. In my use here of the term "reflective reading", I am grouping together a range of different reading moves — critical, suspicious, resistant, or analytic — stemming from various motivations. What they share in common, and what I want to emphasize in bringing them together, is that they all require a reader to stand back from a text to examine it, whether to identify its cultural bias or its use of irony, its ultimate failure or its beauty. Later in this chapter I will more fully examine the necessary and beneficial interaction between the immersive and the reflective modes

of literary reading, but first I want to address the concerns I and these others share about an imbalance in their relationship.

J. Hillis Miller draws a sharp distinction between reading to recreate the alternative world of the text — reading with "innocent, childlike abandonment . . . without suspicion, reservation, or interrogation", a form of reading which requires "a certain speed" (119) — and "slow" or "critical" reading. He writes,

> Slow reading, critical reading, means being suspicious at every turn, interrogating every detail of the work, trying to figure out by just what means the magic is wrought. This means attending not to the new world that is opened up by the work, but to the means by which that opening is brought about. The difference between the two ways of reading might be compared to the difference between being taken in by the dazzling show of the wizard in *The Wizard of Oz* and, on the contrary, seeing the shabby showman behind the façade, pulling levers and operating the machinery, creating a factitious illusion.
>
> (122)

Miller locates this type of "slow" reading in two dominant schools of thought in literary studies: what he calls "rhetorical reading" in which one analyzes the means by which a text works or has its effect, and cultural studies in which one seeks to identify ways in which the culture from which a text emerges shapes that text. Though both approaches to texts undoubtedly make significant contributions to an understanding of literature, Miller observes that "both these forms of critique . . . have as one of their effects depriving literary works, for given readers, of the sovereign power they have when they are read *allegro*" (123). In other words, a reader who interrogates a text will miss out on a full experience of that text's effect.

Miller's observation of this loss in "slow" reading of the power a literary text has when one reads it quickly — when one fully gives oneself over to recreating the alternative world of the text within oneself — leads Miller to make a striking claim. He writes, "No doubt about it, these two forms of critical reading, rhetorical reading and cultural studies, have contributed to the death of literature" (126). How is it that literature has "died"? Miller correlates the rise in "critical reading as demystification" with the fading of literature's "power for cultural indoctrination", as, he observes, "We no longer so much want, or are willing, to be bamboozled by literature" (126). As Miller's choice of terms indicate, literary works have come to be considered less likely to enrapture or enrich their readers, than to "bamboozle" them, a significant shift in the conception of literature. Literary scholars and teachers have long advocated a critical, reflective distance toward texts as necessary for analyzing, interpreting, and evaluating them, ultimately, it has been assumed, as means to facilitate our enrichment by the worthier among literary works. But Miller's account of the practice of critical reading points toward an underlying change in perspective on the role of literature that parallels (or maybe follows from) a shift in the conception of the hermeneutic task that Paul Ricoeur first theorized in a book published some thirty years before Miller's.

In 1970's *Freud and Philosophy*, Ricoeur locates this shift in the works of Freud, Marx, and Nietzsche. In his reading of their works, Ricoeur identifies "the problem of interpretation" as "a new possibility which is no longer either error in the epistemological sense or lying in the moral sense, but illusion," resulting in the use of interpretation "as a tactic of suspicion and as a battle against masks" and the subordination of "the entire problem of truth and error to the expression of the will to power" (*Freud*, 26). In other words, a text (or a dream in the psychoanalytic context or any object of interpretation) is not considered to reveal meaning to its interpreter but to withhold it, to mask it, as an attempt to wield power or maintain control, an attempt Nietzsche, Marx, and Freud, the three "masters" who "dominate the school of suspicion" (*Freud*, 32) would attribute to "the will to power, to social being, to the unconscious psychism" respectively (*Freud*, 34). What I find most striking about this shift in the conception of the task of interpretation is that it assumes that a text is working against its interpreter. Rather than facilitating the communication of meaning, the text obstructs it, requiring the interpreter to become the text's antagonist, to read against the text rather than with it. Of the text and the interpreter, Ricoeur remarks, "*Guile will be met by double guile*" (*Freud*, 34). If a reader lacks sufficient guile, he risks being "bamboozled" by the text. In that case, allowing oneself to become immersed in one's reading of a literary work would be foolishness, submitting oneself to a deception.

Approaching a text with suspicion — meeting it with a greater measure of guile than one expects from it, has become, in Miller's assessment, the attitude underlying the dominant approaches to literary study of recent decades. What has prompted the proliferation of this antagonistic posture toward texts? According to Miller, two motives drive "this effort of demystification". One is "the way literary study . . . is part of the general penchant of our culture toward getting knowledge for its own sake", or ". . . finding out the truth about everything" (124). Finding out the truth about a text — an assumed good in itself — means taking it apart, undoing its workings, demystifying it. The other motive that Miller identifies, he says, "is apotropaic" (125). In other words, undoing the workings of literary texts will help keep us (and our societies) protected from the harm we assume texts will inflict with their power if we allowed them to beguile us and our students.

Another literary scholar, Hans Ulrich Gumbrecht, also recognizes the dominance of the suspicious stance in recent literary study, but offers another account of its provocation in his 2004 book, *Production of*

Presence. In his words, "adopting anything but a 'critical' attitude toward the things of the worlds in which we are living seems to be something like an original sin . . . in the eyes of the average humanist" (92). What is the reason for this attitude? Gumbrecht points to "the loss of world reference and of the dimension of perception during the first decades of the twentieth century" (47), the loss, in other words, of a consistent correspondence between what I perceive and what is real. He posits that the predominance of the "critical" may be a response to "the trauma inflicted" by the "hermeneutically induced . . . 'loss of world'" (92). If a belief in a reliable relationship between perception and reality is no longer possible, then one way of dealing with that loss and the way that dominates the humanities, according to Gumbrecht, is to question everything, to be ever suspicious, vigilant, on guard.

Yet concern over the dominance of the critical or suspicious in academic literary study is also evident in some earlier works in the field as well as these of the last decade. In his 1988 book, *The Company We Keep*, Wayne Booth expresses a similar concern, but points to another cause: the ascendancy in all branches of academia, including the humanities, of the scientific model of the establishment of proof. In the sciences, according to Booth, "true *reason* proceeds by means of critical *doubt* . . . . *Thought* proceeds by critically probing the world's convictions to discover which of them *cannot be doubted*. Only after an opinion has been tested in the fires of doubt can it achieve intellectual respectability" (32, italics original). Booth suggests that literary study of his generation has sought intellectual respectability, securing its place in academia, by imitating the sciences, taking on this model and making doubt primary in its approach to texts.

It may be impossible to determine how accurately any of these explanations accounts for the prevalence of suspicion in approaching texts, if it is prompted by our drive for knowledge for its own sake, our attempt to avoid potential harm, a way of responding to the trauma of our loss of reliable world reference, a quest for intellectual respectability in the broader academic community, or some combination of all of these factors.[9]

---

9 I want to include here some remarks Gabriele Schwab makes in the notes of her book, *The Mirror and the Killer-Queen,* which, I think, suggest another avenue of exploration into conditions underlying the dominance of this antagonistic stance toward objects of study. Because these considerations could take me too far beyond the scope of this project, I only want to raise the issue here and then explore this more fully in another context. What I think Schwab's remarks suggest as an additional factor contributing to the attitude of suspicion in approaching texts is a broad assumption of hostility in all relations with otherness stemming from Lacan and Sartre. Schwab's comments:

Bakhtin's much more positive figuration of otherness posits a subject who finds herself outside. His concept of exotopy requires the other as one who

But what does seem undeniable is what Booth succinctly observes, that the belief that we must begin with doubt "has devastating consequences for criticism of the arts" (32). If the apprehension of a literary text requires an initial act of assent or submission — allowing oneself to become immersed in the world of the text as one imagines it—, then approaching a text with an attitude of suspicion, for whatever reason, will preclude that initial act of temporary self-abandonment or surrender, the essential first step that, in Booth's words, "provides the data with which criticism of narrative deals" (32). To begin with doubt or suspicion, Booth adds, "is simply to destroy the datum" (32). Any act of criticism must come only after one has surrendered to a text; the act of assent, not the position

---

completes the self in a positive and constructive sense. Alienation for Bakhtin would be nearly the inverse of Lacan's or Sartre's alienation: it would lie in the (always impossible) enterprise/fantasy to construct a self independent from the formative impact of the Other. From a Bakhtinian perspective one could read Sartre's and Lacan's texts as cultural symptoms and see this nostalgia for an independent and impermeable subject as an underlying narcissistic fantasy that informs their whole conceptual framework.

(187, note 24)

And from a later note:

In drawing so strongly on the negative predication of otherness on the persecuting gaze of the Other in French theory, some of the more recent theories of culture share their tendency to ontologize destructive historical patterns of cultural contact. And yet, as object relations theories have tried to emphasize against Lacanian psychoanalysis, the gaze of the other is not inherently destructive but becomes so only in an adverse cultural environment. If we essentialize difference (as in the inverse essentialism of some currents in French feminism), or if we ontologize the destruction of otherness in capitalism, colonialism, or even fascism (as in some trends in cultural criticism), then we remain negatively tied to the cultural paranoia that structures the political unconscious of such formations. Ultimately, they are all predicated on escalations of violence against others and on war as the supreme model of cultural relations. The harder it becomes historically to find nondestructive patterns of cultural contact, the more urgent it becomes to envision what such patterns might look like. . . .

Because of the dangers of ontologizing negative cultural histories, we need critically to rethink the potential legacy of cultural paranoia inherited from French and German philosophy, particularly those strands of the tradition that predicate the formation of the subject on a negative, persecuting, and annihilating gaze of the other. The predication of cultural otherness on a persecuting gaze of the other continues to inform many cultural patterns of relating to otherness and perceptions of other cultures in general.

(188, note 26)

of doubt, must be primary.[10] If a reader views a literary work as suspect, as a source of deception or illusion — or bamboozlement — that must be 'out-guiled', she will resist abandoning herself to the recreation of the text's world and will be unable, as Booth implies, to experience the world of the text sufficiently in order to offer any critique (or, at least, a critique Booth would consider of value). Booth confirms what Wilhelm — though at a much more elementary level — observed in his students, that the reflective stance toward a literary text depends upon the initial immersive stance.

What seems in Booth's remarks to be a fairly simple matter of assenting first and doubting later — beginning with immersion in a text and moving to reflection on that text, can in actuality be a challenging move to make. Especially since the beneficial effect of literary reading tends no longer to be assumed, these two modes can imply very contrary views of the text (enriching vs. bamboozling) and call for reading attitudes that seem equally divergent. Walter Slatoff, in his 1970 book, *With Respect to Readers*, makes an observation that is still important for our consideration today as I attempt to work out what can be a difficult interaction between these reading stances. Even before a general mistrust of texts was as prevalent as it has become, he observed that conflicts exist between the approach taken toward a text by a good reader and that taken by a good scholar, producing a tension in academic literary study that he claimed was not sufficiently acknowledged. According to Slatoff, we have tended not to keep in view these conflicts, ". . . the differences between the kinds of detachment, objectivity, narrowing of interest and focus required in scholarship and the kinds of sympathy, engagement, general responsiveness and openness, and emotional susceptibility involved in good reading" (25). The very skills and approach called for in the study of literature tend to be at odds with the qualities necessary for a reader to engage fully with a literary work. That this conflict may still affect students is evident in a comment of one college freshman in a class of mine who, when we were discussing how the students felt about literature, responded that literature is something "to study", as if the requirement of analysis formed the very definition of this type of text.

What for Slatoff was a conflict within literary study has become for J. Hillis Miller, thirty years later, "the aporia of reading" (124). With the emergence in recent decades of suspicion as the dominant stance toward

---

10 I should acknowledge that some measure of assent is required for a reader, even a suspicious reader, to succeed at making any sense at all of a text. As Rosenblatt demonstrates, a reader must allow the text to evoke from her memory images or concepts of some kind if she is to see more than words on paper. My concern here — and Booth's — is the loss of a level of assent beyond that minimal degree necessary for basic sense-making.

texts, these two modes of reading not only pull against one another but, Miller asserts, each "prevents the other from working . . . each inhibits and forbids the other" (124). Their opposition is apparent in Miller's articulation of them, as is the impossibility of holding both attitudes simultaneously. He writes, "How can you give yourself wholeheartedly to a literary work, let the work do its work, and at the same time distance yourself from it, regard it with suspicion, and take it apart to see what makes it tick?" (124). For Miller, the suspicious and the submissive or receptive cannot coexist.

Though Miller draws this dichotomy in perhaps overly stark terms, the insights of all these theorists taken together seem to indicate unquestionably that approaching a text initially from a position of inquiring how it works or, even more so, from the assumption that a text must be read *against* rather than *with* carries with it a deep cost. Miller acknowledges that the "innocent credulity" of his childhood reading experiences may be "irrevocably lost", but he goes on to assert in the final lines of *On Literature* how important that stance toward texts remains if literary reading is going to retain any value. He writes,

> Unless one has performed that innocent first reading, nothing much exists to resist and criticize. The book is deprived beforehand, by a principled resistance to literature's power, of much chance to have a significant effect on its readers. So why read it at all, then, except to satisfy a not wholly admirable joy in destruction, and to keep others from being enraptured, possibly to their detriment? No doubt these resistances to literature have motives quite different from Satan's envy of Adam and Eve's innocent happiness. And yet, are they so different, after all?
>
> (159)

Not only does literary criticism lack its object (or its "datum" in Booth's term) without the reader first submitting himself to the text, but literature itself loses its reason for being read, according to Miller, because it loses its capacity for affecting its readers. If literary works can have no effect, the only motivations Miller claims for literary study are to satisfy a "joy in destruction" and to keep others from being, not bamboozled, but "enraptured", an impetus Miller provocatively locates, through his reference to Milton's Satan, in the scholar's jealousy of the lost pleasures of reading.

Though one need not make as dramatic an accusation as Miller's, one can acknowledge the crucial role of immersing oneself in the imaginary world of the text as one creates it. The reflective mode of reading (whether one expects some form of deception from a text or merely is inquiring into how it works), if it is allowed to dominate or to exclude the immersive mode, will drastically reduce the possibility that a text will become available to a reader as an object in transitional space because the reader is prevented from temporarily abandoning herself to her experience of the object as is necessary for access to this in-between area of experiencing. And this insight has significant implications for literary pedagogy. If we take for granted students' ability or opportunity to create for themselves a world from a text and to immerse themselves in that world so that instruction focuses only on the critical tasks that examine or interrogate that text, we can close off for students the possibility that the text may become an experience capable of facilitating self-formation or of carrying any personal significance at all, reducing it in their estimation to a game or puzzle, an intellectual exercise. Translating the words on the page into a potential object in transitional space depends upon nothing obstructing or interfering with the reader's immersion in the text's world.

That said, a return to my own reading experiences will push this exploration toward one more essential move. Outside of school I've continued to read literature — immersive reading, or, as Miller calls it, reading *"allegro"*, in which I seek what I've experienced as the pleasure of temporarily getting lost in another world. While many of those texts have provided satisfying reading experiences, upon finishing a number of them my response has been, "What was that all about?" That's how I responded to *Moby Dick* (which I somehow missed in my formal literary education) and *To the Lighthouse*, and to a couple of recent novels by Haruki Murakami, and even, to *Beloved*, in spite of a gut-wrenching encounter with the central crisis of that story. My "innocent first reading" provided experiences at times engaging and emotionally moving, but ultimately puzzling, a striking contrast to the deeply powerful connections I experienced with most of the literary texts on which I wrote papers in college and graduate school. In my own reading experience, recreating and immersing myself in the world of the text has at times been unquestionably insufficient to make certain literary texts fully available to me as potential transitional objects (as best I can tell, judging by the strength of my emotional engagement with or attachment to the text and by how much the world of the text stays with me). Or perhaps it might be more accurate to say that through reading *allegro* I was unable to recreate some texts' worlds sufficiently so that I might get lost in them. While a reflective stance toward texts may at times threaten an immersive one, my paper-writing experiences suggest that the worlds of some texts can only be fully recreated and experienced with a significant measure of intentional reflection. This observation certainly won't be "news" to most teachers of literature, but, having attempted so thoroughly to lay out the conflict between these two modes of reading, it is important now to work out more fully their interdependence.

Sustaining the Tension: Immersion and Reflection as Interdependent

It is Paul Ricoeur who offers the fullest exploration I've found of the interdependence of the immersive and the reflective or distancing modes of literary reading. While Ricoeur proposes a fairly stark contrast between the hermeneutics of suspicion which treats double meaning (as in symbols) as dissimulation, and what he calls the hermeneutics of restoration which treats double meaning as revelation (*Freud* 26), he also recognizes that the mode of critique at the heart of the former plays an important role in the latter. He begins to work out that role in *Freud and Philosophy*, furthering that work in later books, including *From Text to Action* (1991), where he claims that "a 'hermeneutics of suspicion' is today an integral part of the appropriation of meaning" (*Text* 100). At the conclusion of the earlier work, Ricoeur attempts a theoretical unification of the two opposing hermeneutics, conceiving of them as co-functions of symbols, in that both shift the origin of meaning to a center outside of consciousness as they simultaneously disguise and disclose, an ambiguity that makes possible the "carrying and engendering" of these "opposed interpretations, each of which is self-consistent" (*Freud*, 496).[11] The reconciliation Ricoeur begins in *Freud and Philosophy* is much more convincingly developed in *From Text to Action*, and it produces a framework useful for thinking about the process of interpretation which focuses on the activity of the interpreter toward the object.

While most would agree that the meaning of a literary text tends not to be immediately apparent, whether one considers a text then to disguise or to disclose that meaning is a matter of perspective which makes a difference in one's attitude or stance toward the text and one's actions with it. A revelation is to be received while a disguise requires interrogation and unmasking. What Ricoeur's reconciliation of these hermeneutics results in is a bringing-together of these modes in a three-stage process starting with a receptive naiveté which passes through a stage of critique and then returns as a second naiveté, this time post-critical and informed but yet "naïve" in its openness or receptivity (*Freud*, 496).

In later works Ricoeur uses the terms "understanding" and "explanation" for these stages, terms he uses not to represent states or things but kinds of interpretive activities which operate dialectically. Understanding both precedes and follows explanation and is a receptive act of synthesis,

---

11 The process through which Ricoeur accomplishes this reconciliation, however, is problematic. He balances what he considers the regression that symbols disguise, based in a psychoanalytic conception of the function of dreams and sublimation, with a progression that symbols reveal. He grounds this view of human progress in a teleological understanding of human life that is difficult to support in the current intellectual climate.

taking in the text as a whole (not in the sense of a completeness or finality, but as undivided). Explanation, on the other hand, is the analytic, critical activity. Ricoeur describes this process, here using the term "comprehension" for the second stage of understanding.

> The first time, understanding will be a naïve grasping of the meaning of the text as a whole. The second time, comprehension will be a sophisticated mode of understanding, supported by explanatory procedures. In the beginning, understanding is a guess. At the end, it satisfies the concept of appropriation, . . . the rejoinder to the kind of distanciation linked to the full objectification of the text. Explanation, then, will appear as the mediation between two states of understanding. If isolated from this concrete process, it is a mere abstraction, an artifact of methodology.
>
> (*Interpretation*, 74–75)

This mediation of understanding by explanation is not only possible but necessary because of the nature of written language. Ricoeur makes clear here that explanation, which involves "the full objectification of the text", serves a supporting role in the approach to texts as it promotes understanding, without which it has no purpose but is "a mere abstraction, an artifact of methodology".

It is within the context of the developing understanding of a text that explanation plays a crucial role. In Ricoeur's words, ". . . explanation has no autonomy. Its advantage and its effect are to allow us to follow the story better and further when the first-order, spontaneous understanding fails" (Text 142). Expanding on this interdependence, Ricoeur adds,

> Strictly speaking, explanation alone is methodical. Understanding is instead the nonmethodical moment that, in the sciences of interpretation, combines with the methodical moment of explanation. This moment precedes, accompanies, concludes, and thus *envelops* explanation. Explanation, in turn, *develops* understanding analytically.
>
> (*Text*, 142, emphasis original)

With these statements, Ricoeur provides an explanation of my own experience with literary works in and out of school. Without a course assignment, I read books for the pleasure of it but lacked the motivation to do the "work" of any kind of analysis, hoping that the text would reveal itself to me in one quick read — the initial naïve understanding, the "guess". But when motivated by a course assignment, I had reason to follow a first reading of a literary work with the effort of a methodical analysis of whatever themes or threads within the story interested me, an act of explanation. This effort produced a dramatically different outcome, as those particular texts became for me weighty, substantial, deeply meaningful experiences which left on me an impact I can still feel.

Of course, what Ricoeur simplifies into a process of three distinct stages will likely involve a much more fluid interaction or oscillation between the receptive and the critical. It may also entail at times many more readings of a text than three. In my own experience, however, the second reading in the mode of explanation did not require yet a third rereading of the text in order to bring about that subsequent "post-critical" understanding (though perhaps another reading would have furthered the effect), but these final two moves seemed to occur almost simultaneously as the insights produced by my analysis instantly pushed forward my grasp of the story in ways that I found immediately and deeply moving. A striking example of this merging of modes and one of my most vivid academic memories occurred as I was writing a paper on Thomas Mann's *Doctor Faustus*. After checking a couple of other dictionaries, I finally found in the oldest one I owned the definition of an obscure word (to me at least) from Mann's novel. The word so perfectly confirmed or fulfilled a theme I'd sensed in the text and had been working to draw out that it brought tears to my eyes, sitting there with the dictionary on my lap, as I felt the literary work further open before me. Even in the moment, I was struck by how something as coldly analytical as a dictionary definition could produce in me such a response.

My efforts of explanation had indeed developed my understanding of the text, resulting in what Ricoeur calls "appropriation" of the text, "when reading yields something like an event, an event of discourse, which is an event in the present moment" (*Interpretation*, 92). An event of discourse, for Ricoeur, recalls the event of one's speaking or listening, actions which are absent or removed from a written text. Appropriating a text through understanding and explanation returns the "event-ness" to the written text as it becomes an experience which I, the reader, recreate and undergo, as I did with Mann's novel. (For Rosenblatt this event, the reader's experience of a text in time, is itself the literary work and the object of literary study.) Some texts that I've read without the effort of analysis have still become "events" for me, but many have not, leaving me with the sense of having missed out on much that the text had to offer.

There is one additional observation I want to make before moving on to the ways in which Ricoeur further develops the interaction between these modes of interpretation. As I mentioned, Ricoeur considers the mode of understanding to be "unmethodical" and only explanation to be "methodical". With pedagogy as the ultimate concern of this project, Ricoeur's assessment has some implications. What is methodical is easier to teach someone to do. What has no method can be prepared for or attested to or perhaps described, but one can't be taught how to do it. That means that what is easier to teach in a literature class only has meaning or value when it is "enveloped" in what can't be easily taught — the receptive "understanding" of a literary work. When literature instruction focuses primarily on the activities of the methodological "explanation", the other stages of reading that should envelope it and thereby give it meaning can be lost to students.

At this point it seems that the role Ricoeur asserts for the critical analytic mode of interpretation is that of a tool, necessary to develop and at times rectify the receptive mode. In *From Text to Action*, he extends much further a conception of the interdependence between the two modes, positing for the critical a much more intrinsic function. He uses as a starting point a debate that runs throughout the work of Hans-Georg Gadamer between "alienating distanciation and the experience of belonging" (*Text*, 70), opposing stances or states notable in their correspondence to the reflective and immersive modes of reading which have been my focus in this chapter. Like a number of other theorists I've mentioned, Gadamer, according to Ricoeur's account, considers belonging to be prior to and foundational for distanciation. Regarding aesthetics, for instance, Ricoeur summarizes Gadamer: ". . . the experience of being seized by the object preceded and renders possible the critical exercise of judgment" (*Text*, 70). Likewise with language: ". . . any scientific treatment of language as an instrument and every claim to dominate the structure of the texts of our culture by objective techniques are preceded and rendered possible by our cobelonging to the things that the great voices of mankind have said" (*Text*, 71). In other words, we must possess or establish some relationship with an object before we can step back and examine that object.

However Ricoeur is not satisfied with Gadamer's description of alienation and belonging because, he claims, it produces an antinomy. In Ricoeur's assessment, Gadamer's conception of alienating distanciation makes possible the objectification that is the method of the human sciences, but at the same time this very objectification "destroys the fundamental and primordial relation whereby we belong to and participate in the historical reality that we claim to construct as an object" (*Text*, 75). Ricoeur then rejects and attempts to overcome this alternative between the "ontological density" of the reality to which we belong and the objectivity of the method which both enables us to examine that reality as it also cuts us off from it. The process by which he does so establishes the centrality of distanciation, in a positive and even productive sense, in written language, leading Ricoeur to call a text "the paradigm of distanciation in communication" in that "it is it is communication in and through distance" (*Text*, 76).

The first level of distanciation that occurs in any instance of language in use is the "distanciation of the saying in the said" — "the surpassing of the event by the meaning" (*Text*, 78). The message being communicated takes on its own existence that extends beyond the act of speaking. Then when an instance of language use is written rather than spoken, its levels of distanciation multiply as it takes on a fundamental autonomy which Ricoeur describes as threefold: "with respect to the intention of the author; with respect to the cultural situation and all the sociological conditions of the production of the text; and finally, with respect to the original addressee" (*Text*, 298). Although still shaped by its original conditions, a piece of writing is in this way freed from them as it can be picked up and read by anyone from any time or place who runs across it. That text will necessarily be "distant" from its reader. As Ricoeur observes, ". . . distanciation is not the product of methodology and hence something superfluous and parasitical; rather it is constitutive of the phenomenon of the text as writing" (*Text*, 84). Distance or alienation can therefore be recognized as "not only what understanding must overcome but also what conditions it", suggesting "a relation between *objectification* and *interpretation* which is much less dichotomous, and consequently much more complementary, than that established by the Romantic tradition" (*Text*, 84), and, I might add, than the "aporia" J. Hillis Miller construes between "innocent" and "critical" reading. According to Ricoeur, "The emancipation of the text constitutes the most fundamental condition for the recognition of a critical instance at the heart of interpretation; for distanciation now belongs to the mediation itself" (*Text*, 298). Because a text, by its very constitution, meets its reader at a distance, overcoming that distance in the process of interpreting the text necessarily requires the critical, analytic mode of explanation. There is never a reception of a text that doesn't entail distanciation. In other words, every reading of a text necessarily involves some critical or reflective activity on the part of the reader.

My own experience of reading aloud to my two children has illustrated for me what Ricoeur has demonstrated so convincingly in theory. The differences I've observed between the three of us as readers make visible the role of critical activity in every act of reading and also point to differences in our awareness of that activity according the abilities and proclivities of readers. The distance Ricoeur identifies as conditioning every text has tended to remain invisible in many of the reading experiences of my older child, Ian, and myself, but it is apparent in my daughter Anna's interactions with the books I read aloud to them. Our reading of the *Harry Potter* series can serve as an example. For me, an experienced reader, these books have proved to be easily engaging, allowing me to dwell temporarily in this imaginary world of which I've admittedly grown very fond, requiring from me almost no attention to the work of decoding words on paper and constructing from them a meaning as the world and the story unfold effortlessly before me. My son, likewise, even as young as three or four, has been able to create without apparent effort a very real world from the words I've read aloud to him. A scene from the first of the Harry Potter books, which he encountered solely through my reading to him as a six-year-old, took shape sufficiently in his imagination to become, regrettably, part of his nightmares. A few years later, as I read an especially suspenseful scene from one of the later books, I will never forget him literally leaping around the room from the intensity of the experience. He "saw" and lived the world of the text as I read it.

My daughter, on the other hand, has been a very different "listener" to books. Although she also considers herself a fan of the Harry Potter stories, it's the movies she initially enjoyed most. Even as a ten- or eleven-year-old, she often remained either only marginally engaged as I read aloud or required frequent pauses in my reading in order that I explain what's going on in the book. Although Anna is an exceptionally bright student, who, for instance, solves complicated math problems in her head for fun, the questions she asked as I read aloud showed that she was not easily able to make the inferences required by literary texts, even ones as relatively "simple" as the Harry Potter books. The gaps in the text that Ian was able to fill without effort even as a very young child were a challenge for Anna, limiting her ability to construct a world from the words I read aloud. The critical activity involved in crossing the distance that is the condition of written text required for Anna much effort. I could help her overcome that distance by periodically returning the text to an event of communication in the present — where I became the speaker addressing her, the audience, in the moment, catching her up on what's going on in the story. It was not that Ian and I need not undertake such critical activities in our reading acts; it was just that for us they were not effortful like they were for Anna and so they were easy to overlook. (Here one might ask if a reading move can still be considered critical when it is effortless or automatic. Regardless of the reader's awareness or effort, a distance must be crossed for a text to mean anything to a reader. The crossing of that distance, however the reader manages it, is my focus here.)

For Anna what was effort-full in reading has gradually become effort-less with continued practice. She could be found laughing her way through some chapter books written at a lower level (the Junie B. Jones series for instance), clearly enjoying the world she was able to create from them, and more recently her own reading of the Harry Potter books has finally surpassed the movies as moving and satisfying experiences in a story world. The nature of effortless reading experiences for Ian continued to expand as well. While listening to me read has long been easy for him, reading the words on the page himself had felt like work until around the time he turned thirteen. After we finished reading the sixth of the Harry Potter books together, he reread on his own the whole series and announced that when the last of the books was finally published he wanted to read it himself. Decoding the words on the page had finally become effortless enough for him that he knew he would be impatient waiting for me to speak the words that he can read more quickly himself.

While all acts of reading require the crossing of distance, I have recognized from my experience reading with my children that the effort involved in that critical or reflective activity will vary considerably among readers according to their individual levels of expertise and, perhaps, inclinations or habits of mind. The effort required of readers to accomplish such activity will also evolve with exposure and practice. As teachers, it can be costly to assume that the process of constructing a world from a text is or should be uniform for all readers.

To return briefly to Ricoeur, there are two other important levels of distanciation that he locates in literary reading. Both of these have to do with his conception of the meaning that a literary text produces — a conception remarkably consistent with the claims of many of the theorists I've discussed thus far regarding the nature of literary reading. For Ricoeur the meaning that a reader seeks from a text is not "an intention hidden behind the text", as in what the author originally meant, but rather is "a world unfolded in front of [the text]" (*Text*, 300), a "world" that is "the ensemble of references opened up by the text" (*Interpretation*, 36). Thus, according to Ricoeur (and in reference to Heidegger), ". . . what we understand first in a discourse is not another person, but a 'pro-ject,' that is, the outline of a new way of being in the world" (*Interpretation*, 37). The task of reading a literary text is therefore "to explicate the type of being-in-the-world unfolded *in front* of the text", drawing forth a "proposed world" that the reader can "inhabit" (*Text*, 86, italics original).

It is this world or way of being in the world proposed by a text that calls for the two additional forms of distanciation that Ricoeur describes. Inhabiting the possible world of a text means setting oneself temporarily at a distance from one's everyday reality, a distance that yields an important opportunity for critique of that reality. This is one way that interpretation of texts "turns toward the critique of ideology" (*Text*, 300), which Ricoeur originally located in the hermeneutic of suspicion. This level of distanciation makes possible the interrogation of one's everyday world from the place of an alternative world which one inhabits temporarily by means of the text.

A similar kind of distanciation becomes possible toward one's self, as well, as a means of advancing self-understanding. In words that recall Gabriele Schwab's reference to the "derealization" of oneself in literary reading, which I mentioned early in this chapter, Ricoeur explains, ". . . just as the world of the text is real only insofar as it is imaginary, so too it must be said that the subjectivity of the reader comes to itself only insofar as it is placed in suspense, unrealized, potentialized . . .. The metamorphosis of the world in play is also the playful metamorphosis of the ego" (*Text*, 300). The possibility of this distanciation of the self from itself within the act of reading further emphasizes the inseparability of explanation from understanding or critique from receptivity. For Ricoeur this "metamorphosis of the ego . . . implies a moment of distanciation in the relation of self to itself," and so "understanding is as much disappropriation as appropriation" (*Text*, 300). As a result, Ricoeur concludes, "The critique of ideology is the necessary detour that self-understanding must take if the latter is to be formed by the matter of the text and not by the prejudices of the reader" (*Text*, 300). In this way Ricoeur makes clear that the state of immersing oneself in a text to such an extent that one temporarily releases one's sense of oneself has at its heart the capacity for critique that I and others had originally opposed to the immersive stance — in this case, the distanciation of oneself from oneself.

What Ricoeur effectively demonstrates, in terms he used earlier, is that any state of belonging neither opposes nor denies an experience of alienation but is necessarily conditioned by it. If we allow ourselves to inhabit the world of a text, we temporarily distance ourselves from our own everyday worlds and even our own selves, a position which enables us to critique our more usual way of being. Literary reading thus makes possible an ideological critique as part of the hermeneutical move of understanding. This capacity for critique carries not only an implied benefit to self and society (the reduction of illusion), but can also be seen as facilitative for literary reading itself because it serves as a "'deconstruction' of prejudices that prevent the world of the text from being allowed to be" (*Text*, 100). In other words, the ideological critique made possible by inhabiting the alternative world of the text at the same time furthers the realization of the text's world as it enables the reader to see past prejudices that would limit her capacity to recreate and enter that world.

Yet there is a form of ideological critique, a way of suspicious reading, that Ricoeur does not address (as far as I can tell). That is the reading that returns to a position of distance from the text in order to critique the ideology within the text itself. For Ricoeur, the critical, analytic stage of explanation operates in the service of understanding the text, of fully appropriating its world, by, on the one hand, a method like structural analysis that makes possible an informed understanding of the text, and, on the other hand, a critique of "prejudices" in the reader's own self and her world that might prevent her from fully recreating the world of the text. But if the world of the text is capable of providing a critique of the "real" world, then surely the "real" world — the reader's world — might also be able to offer a critique of the world of the text. The distance between reader and text makes possible an ideological critique that can move in both directions.

Ricoeur's contribution to my project, and specifically to this chapter as it explores what is necessary for a text to become a transitional object for a reader, comes ultimately in shifting attention from an essentially oppositional relationship between immersive and reflective modes of reading — in Ricoeur's terms, receptive understanding and distancing explanation — to the productive interdependence between them. Ricoeur's articulation of this turn in the context of hermeneutics, from which his own interrogation proceeds, I think is equally significant within the context of pedagogy. He writes, "Would it not be appropriate to shift the initial locus of the hermeneutical question, to reformulate the question in such a way that a certain dialectic between the experience of belonging and alienating distanciation becomes the mainspring, the key to the inner life, of hermeneutics?" (*Text*, 297). Likewise, might a dialectic between immersing oneself in a literary work (as is necessary for its formative use) and standing back to reflect on that work (as seems necessary for a fuller immersion) become "the mainspring, the key to the inner life" of literary pedagogy?

As in any dialectic, the tension which can be so productive can also be difficult to maintain as attention tends to fall toward one or the other pole, idealizing one and vilifying or ignoring the other. Just such a breakdown may explain at least in part the challenges Jeffrey Wilhelm faced with his middle-school remedial readers. When the focus of instruction is solely on the method of reading — that which can be more easily be taught, in this case phonics drills and comprehension questions — the nonmethodical which gives the method its meaning is lost by neglect, and reading becomes little more than a mystifying, empty exercise. This sometimes uneasy interdependence between immersion and reflection — belonging and distanciation, the "innocent" and the critical — which Wilhelm encountered in its breakdown, is already a part of the pedagogical thought of one teacher of literature and teacher educator, Deanne Bogdan. Her insights into this dialectic, derived from both the convergence and the dissonance between her study of Northrop Frye and her years of experience in post-secondary literature classrooms, form a fitting conclusion to this hefty chapter as they return us to the pedagogical context which is my primary concern.

Bogdan's book, *Re-Educating the Imagination: Toward a Poetics, Politics, and Pedagogy of Literary Engagement*, both helpfully elaborates on the interdependence between the immersive and reflective modes of reading as it also offers an additional — and significant — complication. Analogous to Ricoeur's conception of the roles of understanding and explanation, the dialectic Bogdan posits as necessary to a "full" literary response is the "alternation between engagement, or the participating response, and detachment, or the critical response" (119). She emphasizes, with Frye, the importance of the "aesthetic distance" of the critical mode in moving students beyond "stock responses", which Bogdan describes as "passive forms of automatic reflex, reinforcing what is already known rather than paving the way for what might be known" (116). More obviously incomplete than naïve understanding in Ricoeur, a stock response, originally conceptualized by I. A. Richards, is a reader's reaction to a text that is informed less by her attention to the text itself than to her reaction to some aspect of the content or form of the text based in some preconception or assumption of her own. Frye prioritizes critical detachment over participation in the text because of the inadequacy of this incomplete response, but Bogdan disagrees, informed by her experiences with students. For Bogdan, the dialectic in literary response between engagement and detachment "legitimates and capitalizes on" partial or incomplete responses "by building on whatever emotional and intellectual raw material presents itself at a precritical level, and in such a way that response can be deepened, refined, and enriched through aesthetic distance" (119). In the context of a literature classroom, the naïve understanding of Ricoeur's formulation and the "innocent" reading of Miller's may in fact be the first readings students produce that can often seem so sadly wrong-headed to most teachers of literature. Rather than attempting to avoid such apparent failures — to prevent students from such wrong-headedness — Bogdan recognizes the value of these precritical readings to literary instruction as the starting points on which to build. In light of Ricoeur's claims about critical explanation's dependence on the initial mode of understanding, students' first readings, however wayward, are essential if the critical activities we ask of them are to have any meaning or value for them. Even when their initial encounters with a text are determined more by their own preconceived notions than by anything arising from the text itself, it is with those reading attempts that instruction must begin because that is where the student is.

Starting from the situations and conditions of the real and diverse students in any given literature classroom carries another implication, which forms the heart of Bogdan's book, and it is one that's crucial for literary pedagogy and also for this discussion of the formative use of literature. A classroom of students were the means by which Bogdan came to this realization, specifically the students in the first course in feminist criticism that Bogdan's institution offered. Halfway through the course, Bogdan decided to use Updike's short story, "A & P", to examine "how the aesthetic mechanism intersects with female stereotyping" (140), but one student challenged the very presence of the story in the course on feminism, arguing, in Bogdan's words, that in their brief time together "the class could not afford to learn how yet again sexism gets rationalized within a masculinist poetics" (141). When Bogdan asked what then should be done with such a text, this student replied and some others concurred, "I am not a censor, but burn the damned thing!" (141). Here is Bogdan's account of the reflection this student's response provoked:

> . . . I'd hoped to demonstrate just how the dialectical working
> through of the sexist biases in the story . . . could ultimately neutral-
> ize the story's offensiveness. In face of the call to "Burn the damned
> thing!" I lost any hope of moving my students from engagement to

detachment in a single evening. In fact, since then I have realized that the very polarization of these two states masks a false dichotomy in modes of literary response, a dichotomy that trivializes the intuitive and privileges the ratiocinative, which denigrates readers' tacit knowledge in favor of critics' "objectivity." While there is always somewhere to go in criticism, one can only be where one is.

(148)

In valuing readers' tacit knowledge and starting from where the student is in approaching texts (the only place one can be, as Bogdan points out), this teacher encountered an unexpected obstacle as she sought to move students from their initial reactions to a more informed (and detached) analysis. These students in this context rejected this text outright.

Their refusal draws attention to a risk intrinsic to the distanciation that Ricoeur identifies at the heart of literary reading, the distanciation of one's self from itself (like the temporary loss of self definition that is transitional experience). The needs of particular students (or, more generally, particular readers) in particular contexts can prevent them from being able or willing to "derealize" themselves in their reading, the loosening of self boundaries that is necessary in the self-expansion or reformation that is a "good" of literary reading. Readers' real positions in life may challenge what Bogdan calls "the poetics of pluralism" or reading literature to experience other lives and perspectives. In her experience with these students and this story, Bogdan realized that the "need" of a feminist criticism class "to preserve their identity" precluded, in her words, "magnanimity as a first priority", leading her to conclude: "The poetics of pluralism is contingent upon a certitude of identity that comes with being in power rather than out of power, individually and/or collectively" (143).

If readers lack the "certitude of identity" that comes from a position of relative power, then releasing themselves to enter into the alternative world of a literary text can become too great a risk. As Bogdan later explains, "When my identity is comparatively free from threat, my reading ego can be more expansive, and I can embrace the unknown with a minimum of psychic risk." To illustrate, she adds, "If, however, I have just been sexually accosted in the subway station, the radiant regency of my reading ego in a story replete with sexist images might well be "regressed" from an attitude of aesthetically living-through the story to one of fight or flight" (187–88). The situations of some readers (both inner states and outer circumstances) can cause their immersion in the worlds of some texts to be actually traumatizing and therefore to be defended against "by fight or flight". At the same time, it's important to acknowledge that the expansion of the self's boundaries will necessarily at times bring discomfort. In experiences that we choose for ourselves, it can sometimes be difficult to distinguish between a needed and ultimately beneficial discomfort and a provocation that pushes too far, becoming truly harmful. How much more difficult it is to make such determinations in what we ask of our students.

Bogdan's insight into the effect of the real-life positions of particular readers on the process of literary reading adds another valuable component to the distanciation that Ricoeur sees as intrinsic to the text because it is written. In Bogdan's class on feminist criticism, distanciation between reader and text in the form of a critique of the ideology of the text emerges (the form of ideological critique Ricoeur does not discuss in *From Text to Action*), not as a "product of methodology and hence something superfluous and parasitical", to borrow Ricoeur's words, but as a spontaneous reaction against offense and threat. Recalling Miller's terms, in some cases it is indeed crucial that certain readers are not willing to be "bamboozled" by certain works of literature, as means of self-protection. While this critique would be made more substantial by the reflection of a careful analysis (of both the text and the reader's self), it bears value in its immediacy for the perspective it offers of the text in question and of the process of literary reading itself. As Bogdan emphasizes, the transformative capacity of literary reading can bring ill instead of good for particular readers of particular texts in particular contexts. Bogdan is wise to remind us that when real readers meet literary texts which invite, as she says, the "fluidity of boundaries between self and the world, ordinary existence and imaginative experience, consciousness and repression of consciousness, identity and loss of identity", the reading experience becomes "fraught with the potential for the kind of destabilizing that student readers may neither expect nor welcome, depending on where they might be in terms of feeling, power, and location, especially in a classroom" (192). She adds, "By continuing, nevertheless, to press for this kind of engaged reading, teachers of literature are burdened with an awesome responsibility . . ." (192), a responsibility which, in light of my claims in this inquiry, should stay at the forefront of our minds. The distance at which some students will keep some texts may consciously or unconsciously be their sole protection against a potentially transformative encounter with a text that could prove to be more than they could psychically bear at the time. As teachers we must tread lightly through such vulnerable territory, respecting students' varying capacities for destabilization while also challenging them to take risks with texts.

Having been reminded of the very real risks for readers of engaging with literary texts, I want to return finally to the question with which I began this chapter. What does it take for a text to become a transitional object for a person who reads it? Or, in other words, what does the activity of reading entail that makes a story or poem available to a reader for use in transitional space? Drawing on the insights of all of these theorists, one can say that this formative use of literature requires that a reader construct from the text a world in her imagination into which she can immerse herself, allowing herself to get lost in the world of the text as she is absorbed in the experience, and her sense of self and her sense of the text's world temporarily merge. This immersive mode is the heart of literary reading as it becomes the reader's experience of the world of the text, but it is not universal or automatic for all who read — who can decode the words on the page. For some it must be learned or prompted, a need literature instruction must not overlook.

Also essential to literary reading, but in a supporting role, is reflective or critical reading, reading at a distance. Critical reading, to adapt one of Ricoeur's claims, *develops* immersive reading, while immersion *envelopes* (and gives meaning to) the critical. A reader steps back from the text to analyze aspects of it in order to recreate its world more fully. And he can use distance from the text to evaluate its world in comparison with his own, as he can also question the means by which the text works or has its effect. While the reflective mode is meaningless without the immersive, the immersive without the reflective is insufficient or ultimately impossible since all texts necessarily entail a distance from the original event of communication. Bridging that distance necessitates some reflective activity, though it may have become effortless for the reader and therefore goes unnoticed.

The challenge comes in that these two modes of approach, while dependent on one another, also pull against one another and so can be difficult to hold together. This is especially true in the context of schooling. When critical reading receives primary or even exclusive emphasis in literary education — either intentionally because texts are viewed as ultimately deceptive, bamboozling readers, or unintentionally because the immersive mode of reading is taken for granted and neglected — then the heart of literary reading can be lost for students. With that heart is also lost the potential formative use of literary texts. Essential then to literary education is ensuring that a place is made in the classroom and in the conception of reading that students take from the classroom for the immersive mode of reading. Before making recommendations to that end, I want to examine some descriptions of recent practices in literary education in light of these concerns.

3 Recent Conceptions of Literary Education and Their Potential Impact on Students' Formative Use of Literature

At this point in my endeavor to establish a conception of the value of literary reading that can inform teaching, I am now able to return explicitly to the matter of pedagogy. In Chapter 1, I claimed that the reading of literary texts has value for individuals and for societies as an opportunity for needed alterations of conceptions of self and other through the use of texts as objects in transitional space. Then, in Chapter 2, I sought to demonstrate that this formative work requires that readers immerse themselves in the world of the text as they also stand back from that world at times during the process of reading for reflection and critique, a dialectic relationship that can be difficult to maintain. Before offering some pedagogical recommendations that these ideas entail, which will form the focus of my final chapter, I first want to examine recent approaches to literary instruction by means of texts on the teaching of literature. My purpose is to evaluate their potential effect on students' capacity to make use of literary texts as transitional objects and also to identify any insights or challenges they might suggest toward the development of a pedagogy conducive to the formative use of literature.

As I've asserted, the use of a literary text as an object in transitional space cannot directly be taught — one cannot be shown how to do it — because it is a largely unconscious process, but what a literature course does teach are ways of reading that might either invite or spoil opportunities for such use. Furthermore, a teacher's conception of the nature of literary instruction will itself shape students' perspectives on literature — what they realize they can do with texts. Therefore, in this chapter, I will take up the questions of how literary instruction is conceptualized in texts on teaching literature of the last couple of decades, and also how the reading and study of literature are conceived in those texts, looking specifically for indications of their potential impact on students' capacity to use literary texts as transitional objects. The texts I have examined for this study were published in the past several decades and focus on the post-secondary teaching of literature, with the addition of a few works for high school teachers that make particular contributions to this inquiry. Also, some of these are edited volumes and so represent the views of some twenty to thirty instructors each, giving added breadth and a challenging variety to the pedagogical approaches I'll attempt to gather here.

Before proceeding I want to acknowledge a problem that necessarily limits the nature of the claims I can make in this examination: the inevitable discrepancy between educators' written accounts of their teaching principles and practices and what actually transpires in their classrooms and in their students' learning. My examination of literature instruction in this study focuses on what teachers have written to describe their intentions and their methods for the literature courses they teach. While there is no reason to accuse these educators of being in any way disingenuous, it is important to remember that an instructor is able to offer only her own perspective of a learning event (and inevitably a somewhat idealized one at that). Even when she might choose to give voice to students' perspectives by including direct quotations from them, as does Jeffrey Wilhelm, whom I discussed in the previous chapter, the perspective of the texts as a whole is, of course, ultimately still that of the author. While one individual's perspective on any event is not a consistently reliable reflection of what others might have perceived or experienced, it is nevertheless informative and therefore valuable as one form of evidence, but a necessarily partial one. One of these books on literary pedagogy makes this discrepancy especially clear as it balances teachers' descriptions of their instructional approach with researchers' observations of what transpired in those classrooms, and it offers an important reminder of the limits of my method. Although this particular text reports on several studies conducted largely among secondary students and classrooms, its findings are informative as well for the post-secondary context, where my interest lies.

In *The Language of Interpretation: Patterns of Discourse in Discussions of Literature*, Marshall, Smagorinsky, and Smith report the findings of a number of studies they conducted on the ways students talk about literary texts both inside and outside of secondary classrooms. After interviews with students and teachers, and observation of several literature classrooms, they come to some surprising findings that present an important caution to any assertions drawn only from teachers' accounts of their practices and principles. Consistently across the classrooms they observed, there was a noticeable gap between what teachers intended their students do and what students actually did. Marshall, Smagorinsky, and Smith write, "While the goal expressed by teachers was to help students toward a point where they could individually develop a response to the text, we saw in the classrooms we observed few occasions where students could practice such interpretive skills, at least during large-group discussions" (56). As a result of tensions like this between what teachers wanted to see their students do and what students were able or willing to perform, the researchers observed "a move away from the student-centered discussions the teachers saw as ideal toward the teacher-dominated discussions that most hoped to avoid" (30). Students' lack of participation in the practices that teachers hoped for resulted in an enactment of more traditional teacher-student roles in the classroom that these particular teachers had hoped to avoid. These teachers' "belief that discussions should emerge from students' interests and flow with the authority of students' voices was rarely embodied in the actual discussions that took place in their classrooms" (131). The instructional approach that teachers valued in their talk about their teaching was not evident in what these researchers observed actually taking place in their classrooms. As I turn to recent texts on post-secondary literature instruction, it is important to keep in mind that they consist entirely of instructors' accounts of their teaching approaches without the additional perspective of an outsider's observation of classroom activities, and so are not necessarily accurate indicators of what actually transpires in their literature classrooms. They do, however, provide informative, though somewhat idealized, perspectives on conceptions of literary education.

In her book on the teaching of literature, Elaine Showalter claims, ". . . all of us who teach literature believe that it is important not only in education but in life" (24). While it is likely that those who teach literature do agree that it is important, and therefore that their work has value, the agreement may end there. Showalter goes on to acknowledge the difficulty the profession has in defining its work. She writes, "Among the more abstract sources of our present anxieties is our inability to articulate a shared vision of our goal that can provide a sense of ongoing purpose and connection" (24).[1] This lack of a shared goal, or a shared conception of what teaching literature means, could not be more apparent in works on the subject. As illustration, a collection edited by Tanya Agathocleous and Ann Dean, *Teaching Literature: A Companion*, presents an array of amazingly diverse formulations of teaching, including descriptions of practices as varied as this by Carolyn Williams: "I begin by introducing rhetorical or grammatical figures of self-reflection, and then move rapidly toward the consideration of narrative structure; finally, I emphasize form

---

1 Interestingly, Showalter proposes making pedagogy itself a focus that might unify the profession. She writes, "Attention to pedagogy itself, and to learning theory, could offer a new direction for English studies for the new century. Whether or not we can offer a rigorous definition of 'literature', we could make teaching it our common cause, and teaching it well our professional work" (24). Though teaching well should indeed be a primary concern of all teachers of literature, Showalter's proposal overlooks the problem of determining what teaching well means when there is no agreement on what the teaching is meant to accomplish.

as it relates to genre" (12–13), and this by Richard Miller: "Thus, instead of arguing about which reading was right, my students would research the ways the novel had been read and ask [among other questions]: what makes certain ways of reading available to some readers and not to others?" (132). The volume's pedagogical advice offers even more variety, from Nancy Henry's recommendation to project a good map of England on a screen in teaching Victorian literature (50), to Charles Altieri's treatise on the affective function of lyric poetry as a guide for teaching it.

While the widely varied conceptions of literary education emerging from these texts can appear haphazard, some trends in approach emerge, trends that represent the instructional models generally available in the field of literary education. Literary instruction, as it's articulated in a number of these pedagogical texts, consists largely of the instructor's activity, which students observe or in some way receive. In other cases, literary education is a matter of engaging students themselves in some form of activity with texts. I will use these broad generalizations to give structure to this chapter as I explore theoretically the potential effect of these approaches on students' capacity to make formative use of literature.

Literary Education as the Instructor's Activity

While it has served as a valuable source for literature instructors for several decades, the Modern Language Association's series, Approaches to Teaching World Literature, largely demonstrates this tendency to focus exclusively on the instructor's actions in a literature classroom. In fact many of the essays in the volumes I read make little mention of students at all. A selection from *Approaches to Teaching Achebe's Things Fall Apart* provides an example of this tendency. In his essay in the volume, Ousseynou Traoré writes, "To *illustrate a typical class discussion*, I conclude this essay with a matrical analysis of an epic paradigm that describes a significant aspect of Okonkwo's character: the fragment of Umuofia's foundation myth embedded in the novel's first paragraph" (69, italics added). What follows is just what one might expect of an analysis of an epic paradigm as a matrix. But how does an analysis such as this, with no reference to students or teachers or any speakers at all, illustrate a class discussion? We can clearly assume that for Traoré a "class discussion" must be synonymous with an instructor's lecture and that the analysis his essay offers must serve as the content of that lecture — what the instructor would say to the students.

A statement from another essay from this same volume does make reference to students, but at the same time makes clear who in the class is the "actor" or agent. Of his instructional approach, Simon Gikandi writes,

> My major task in introducing students to *Things Fall Apart* is to provide a theoretical foundation for relating Achebe to his times

without discussing his novel simply as an empirical record of Igbo culture or the African experience before and during the period of colonization. My goal is not to deny the validity of Achebe's claims about the sources of his novel but to complicate his pronouncements on culture and representation.

(26)

It is objectives like this one, focused largely on what the teacher does, that seem to be the norm in most of the volumes I examined from the MLA Approaches to Teaching series.[2] Admittedly, Gikandi's and Traoré's intentions for their students likely extend beyond their merely knowing about the function of cultural representation in Achebe's novel or an "epic paradigm" embedded within it. For them it may go without saying that they intend their work in the classroom to serve as a model according to which students will pattern their own reading practices. Nevertheless, their accounts of their teaching approaches make no mention of attempts to develop in students the textual skills these instructors demonstrate. Gikandi's essay, like Traoré's, consists largely of a recounting of what he says to his students about Achebe's novel, in statements like this: "By this time, of course, I find myself discussing Achebe and the narrator as if they were interchangeable. My final lecture on the novel seeks to complicate the relation between author and narrator before I raise the issues of voice and representation which are crucial to understanding the novel" (30). In leaving unmentioned their expectations for what their students will be able to do with the information given them or what value it offers them, these authors take for granted the assumptions of the readers of their pedagogical essays about what literature courses like theirs should make possible for students.

In another of the volumes I read, *Approaches to Teaching Eliot's Poetry and Plays*, this tendency to construe the instructor as the primary actor in the classroom is even more pronounced. In fact, of the twenty-five essays on Eliot's poetic works in the volume, only six suggest any kind of specific instructional practices — what teachers might have students do or might do with them in a class. Of the other nineteen, a few make no mention of students or teacher, course or classroom, at all, while others mention students only in an introductory or concluding reference, the bulk of each of these essays offering a critical perspective on the text under consideration.

---

2 I selected four of the volumes of the MLA's Approaches to Teaching World Literature series to examine in depth, chosen for the varied literary periods they address and for their dates of publication spread over the much of history of the series: 1980's volume on Chaucer's *Canterbury Tales*, 1988's volume on Eliot's poetry and plays, 1991's volume on Achebe's *Things Fall Apart*, and 2002's volume on English Renaissance drama.

To consider these essays as offering an approach to teaching requires us to presume that their authors advocate either saying these things to students in a course on Eliot or perhaps that these perspectives are somehow crucial for a competent teacher of Eliot to bear in mind as she teaches her subject. In Agathocleous and Dean's volume on teaching literature, Nancy Henry succinctly articulates (and recommends) this conception of literary education when she writes of teaching the literature of any historical period, "The key is to know the material and to convey your knowledge to the students . . ." (55).

While the lecture as primary mode of instruction, with the passive role it requires of students, has been a common object of critique in recent years, I want to address the conception of literary education these texts exhibit — a matter of the instructor conveying information to students through lecture — from the perspective of my interest in making literary texts available for formative use. In its emphasis on the content of a course — the body of information to be conveyed, these descriptions of literature instruction leave the consideration of method unaddressed and invisible, both the method of teaching and the method of reading. In both areas, the process or the "how-to" is assumed to be natural or inevitable. If reading is assumed to be a homogenous, transparent, and relatively universally mastered process among college students, and therefore deserving of little attention, then what students need from a college literature course is only the specialized knowledge that reading more sophisticated literary texts require. If the task of teaching is likewise considered to be an unproblematic conveyance of information or insight from teacher to student, then little thought is given to the questions of how students process what they take in and what they do with the information they receive or are assumed to receive. The question of how one can then tell that learning is actually taking place doesn't come up, nor does the question of what that learning is meant to accomplish — at least not in these essays on approaches to teaching particular texts.

Although conceiving of education as a simple act of conveying information is problematic in any subject area, it presents a notable potential obstacle to the formative use of literature. If the activity in the classroom is largely the teacher's, his lectures about particular texts will model for students not only what can be done with a literary text, but what should be done. As evident in the two examples I mentioned above, the material to be covered in literature courses taking this approach is almost exclusively focused on the analytical, critical, distancing mode of reading, the mode which undoubtedly requires specialized knowledge of some kind. As a result, the other mode and the one essential to the formative use of literature — when one immerses oneself in the world of the text — can easily remain invisible. If students have not already discovered and experienced immersive reading for themselves — and

Wilhelm's research among middle school students suggests that earlier stages of schooling can also tend to exclude this reading stance — then its neglect in post-secondary literature classrooms will only further this deficiency. Literary reading for these students can remain a meaningless exercise if they have not discovered the world-making capacity of literary texts. Certainly, forms of specialized knowledge can prove to be the key that opens up the worlds of some literary works for some students, but many do not succeed at making this turn, according to the observations of the experienced teachers of literature I cited in the introduction, Walter Slatoff, A. D. Moody, and Sheridan Blau, who attest to little evidence in their students' written work and class discussion of meaningful engagement with texts.

However, not all who conceive of literary education as primarily the instructor's activity neglect in their instructional approach — at least theoretically — the more immersive mode of reading that gives experiential or felt meaning to the critical. A notable example is Cleanth Brooks whose essay, written late in his professional life, on teaching Eliot's "The Love Song of J. Alfred Prufrock" draws attention to the context within which knowledge about a text takes on significance. Brooks emphasizes that students "must appropriate the poem for themselves" and that the "poem as a total experience is the important thing" (78–79). Reading poems like Eliot's, Brooks claims, does requires special knowledge, but he adds this caution: "Yet simply to possess the knowledge does not suffice. Students need to know what to do with such information, just how it bears on the main theme and what emotional weight it deserves to bear . . . .. Such knowledge, even if discovered through scholarly diligence, may result in nothing more than a heap of learned glosses on particular lines" (79). Clearly Brooks believes that a literary education should result in a students' ability to read a poem in such a way that they make it their own, that they enter into it as "a total experience".

Then how does Brooks help them to do so? The rest of Brooks' essay consists of a description of his reading of "Prufrock", including the special knowledge required. So Brooks appears to conceive of his role in the literature classroom as delivering that knowledge as he also models how to read the poem, but it seems that he then leaves the students to work out on their own how to appropriate the poem for themselves. Brooks' students bear the responsibility for transforming his demonstration into something more for them than just "a heap of learned glosses on particular lines". Although Brooks clearly seems to recognize the insufficiency of an exclusive focus on the transmission of knowledge in literary education to the neglect of students' appropriation of texts, it appears in his account of teaching Eliot's "Prufrock" that his conception of literary instruction places the activity in the classroom with the instructor and not the students. Therefore it remains unclear whether students will be better able to make use of literary texts as transitional objects as a result of an instructional approach like Brooks' because there is no indication, at least in Brooks' essay, of how students are helped to enact a reading of their own.

When the instructor is assumed to be the primary actor in the class-room, students' learning is left up to them to work out. Rather than learners, students become, as Sheridan Blau observes, "merely witnesses" to their instructor's learning. "What they would know, therefore," Blau explains, referring to himself delivering a lecture, "was that I had learned it, and their notes would record some of what I had learned. But the experience of learning was mine, not theirs" (2). Robert Scholes articulates a distinction in conceptions of the objective of teaching that can help remedy this deficiency when he writes, "Our job is not to produce 'read-ings' for our students but to give them the tools for producing their own" (*Textual Power*, 24). A number of teachers of literature offer, in their writ-ings, conceptions of literary education that explicitly endeavor to involve students actively in producing "readings", through both giving them necessary "tools" and requiring students to put those tools to use. How these instructional approaches can affect students' potential formative use of literary texts is a question in need of some investigation.

Literary Education in Which Students Are Actively Involved

Before looking at these other approaches to literary instruction, I want to consider further a concern about approaches that casts students in a pas-sive role. Underlying this classroom phenomenon may be a pedagogical error that Scholes identifies: "the equation of coverage with knowledge" (*Rise and Fall*, 148). It can be easy to assume that "covering" the material ought to be sufficient for students to "know" the material, but, as Scholes points out, "Knowledge that is not usable and regularly used is lost. The knowledge we retain is the knowledge that we can and do employ" (*Rise and Fall*, 148). Not only can what is used be better retained, but so can what is *useful*. Scholes advocates reconceptualizing literary instruction as focused on "the process of reading" rather than "coverage of texts" (*Rise and Fall*, 166), since, as he claims, the coverage model "does not reach students effectively because they do not know why they need it", and, even more significantly, it is in many cases "not what they need most" (*Rise and Fall*, 157). In other words, education as coverage requires that students themselves process or appropriate the information presented yet without making apparent to them a reason to do so — aside from their need to perform well on an exam, of course. Scholes even moves a step further here by suggesting that not only do students in a coverage-model classroom tend to see little need for the literary knowledge they are asked to master, they may in fact have insufficient need for it, as other needs they have take precedence. (Later in this chapter I will examine what

Scholes claims students do need from a literary — or, more broadly, a textual — education.)

Similar to the shift in the focus of literary education from coverage to knowledge-in-use that Scholes advocates is Elaine Showalter's recommendation that we "teach reading literature as a craft, rather than as a body of isolated information" (26). In her book, *Teaching Literature*, Showalter offers a goal for a literary course of study that focuses entirely on what students will be able to *do*. She writes, "Overall, our objective in teaching literature is to train our students to think, read, analyze, and write like literary scholars, to approach literary problems as trained specialists in the field do, to learn a literary methodology, in short to 'do' literature as scientists 'do' science" (25). While the objective of literary education she puts forward indeed emphasizes student learning in terms of skills or knowledge-in-use, it raises the question of that learning's usefulness to most students. Apart from those who plan to become literary scholars or teachers of literature themselves, do students have a need for the skills of a literary scholar? What is the use of these skills for most students? To this question Showalter proposes a provisional answer: "But we could say that we want students to learn a set of critical reading skills they can apply to the world of language, literature, and culture around them throughout their lifetime" (26). In other words, Showalter suggests, the literary scholar's skills are useful for understanding the world around us, and so are worth teaching students. But this application of the craft of literary reading receives only a relatively brief acknowledgement in her description of literary study's objectives while the bulk of her book remains focused on the teaching of literature apparently as an end in itself, leaving students to work out for themselves how to use their newly acquired skills outside of the classroom.

Showalter recognizes that this shift in emphasis from knowledge to skill development as the objective of literary education requires a comparable shift in teaching methods. Regarding the teaching of poetry, for instance, she observes, "Lecturers can present, explain, and demonstrate the subject matter of poetic analysis and interpretation, but telling the students about it is not the same as involving them in it" (68). Her book, however, provides only rather brief examples of how to do so. As a gathering together of the insights and practices of many experienced teachers of literature, Showalter's book does not present a single, thoroughly developed instructional approach. The variety of perspectives offered indeed makes this a valuable resource for new teachers of literature, but leaves it difficult to anticipate the potential effects of Showalter's conception of literary education for making literary texts available to students as transitional objects. Shifting attention, as Showalter does, from the presentation of a body of knowledge to the development of students' abilities to read and study literature will increase the likelihood that students will have experiences of their own with texts, but an emphasis on the scholarly practices of criticism and analysis may marginalize more immersive modes of reading.

Scholes, who also advocates that students acquire through literature courses an active useful knowledge and the ability to put it to use, provides a description of his instructional approach that makes clear that he asks students to take an active part in what transpires in the class and suggests the means by which he does so. He chooses the texts students read and guides their attention by the focus of the questions he asks them, but, according to his account, it is their responses to his questions that are the observations, the connections, the perspectives that become the "readings" produced in class. Though I will later discuss the particular objectives Scholes proposes for a "useful" literary education, here I would like to mention as illustration of his instructional method a few of the specific questions or tasks he asks of students. After having students read a short story, Scholes says he begins by asking "where this text becomes a story" (*Textual Power*, 26). In another instance, Scholes asks students, after reading a story, "to make explicit the ways that they construct a scene, a world, from the words on the page, starting with particular words . . ." (*Textual Power*, 27). And then in response to a story which includes a number of different sections, he asks students "to describe or characterize the narrative voice or presence that we encounter in each of the six sections" (*Textual Power*, 68). Each of these inquiries require students to become more aware of the way a story works, not by listening to Scholes' conclusions about the question but through making observations and developing conclusions of their own. Interestingly, each of these questions also pushes students to attend to the world-making quality of literary texts and to their experiences of the worlds they construct as readers of texts. In reflecting on the differences in narrative presence between sections of a text, for instance, students must notice how the world or the perspective of each section felt to them. As he asks students to reflect on their reading experiences, Scholes makes room in class for a more immersive reading mode by putting to students questions whose answers depend upon such reading.

Like Scholes' account of his instructional approach, and in contrast to most of the essays in the other volumes of the MLA's Approaches to Teaching series I reviewed, many of the essays in 2002's *Approaches to Teaching English Renaissance Drama* describe students as taking an active part in a literature course. The treatment of students' roles in this volume may be an outcome of the recognition among teachers of drama of the importance of performance in understanding and appreciating this genre, but the nature of the genre itself doesn't fully account for the approach the text's editors take. In their introduction to the volume, editors Karen Bamford and Alexander Leggatt, offer an articulation of their objectives for a course in their subject that remains notably focused on the students and mindful of the usefulness of their subject of study. They intend that students through a course on Renaissance drama "[get] in touch with a culture radically different from ours" and that students realize "that for all [Renaissance dramas'] initial strangeness, there is much that we can recognize in the images of life they offer". They add, "Finally, having got to know [the texts], we return to our own world, able to look at it with fresh eyes, as one looks at one's own country with fresh eyes after having been away from it for a while" (xi). Why study Renaissance drama? So that students can gain perspective on their own world by getting out of it for a time and into a world very distant from their own, an opportunity for contact with a culture separated from theirs by centuries. In their conception of the objective of a course on this subject, Bamford and Leggatt seem to consider temporarily immersing oneself in the world of the text to be at the heart of what should transpire. But how can students be enabled to accomplish such a feat?

While the accounts of instructional approaches in all nine of the essays in the "Strategies" section of this Approaches to Teaching volume place students in an active role, two of them include such thorough pictures of ways their authors work to aid their students in getting "in touch" with the world of Renaissance dramas that they are worth a detailed look. In the first of these essays, "'Our Sport Shall Be to Take What They Mistake': Classroom Performance and Learning", Helen Ostovich understands her own role as instructor to be "to achieve a classroom situation" that provokes her students to rethink their own understandings of drama and of past and present (87). How does she create such a situation? The rethinking her students accomplish comes as they themselves struggle in small groups to prepare performances of portions of the plays they read. Their efforts to work out an interpretation of the text, including staging, costumes, props, and sets, and then their analysis of their response to their own and their classmates' performances, together become the means by which they learn about Renaissance drama and get "in touch" with another very distant culture. Ostovich helpfully uses two pages of her essay to explain specifically how she sets up the tasks she asks students to undertake, and then the remaining four pages to describe particular instances that have occurred in classroom performances and the realizations they've elicited as illustrations of outcomes of her approach. Creating a dramatic presentation from the words on the page requires that students visualize a world from the text, pushing them through the challenge of making some sense of such a long-ago culture. Likewise, performing that drama means students become its characters temporarily and requires putting themselves into the world of the text. And then watching the performances of other groups in the class gives the added benefit of seeing how others undertook the process of creating a world from a text, making visible differences in their process and in its product. Although, with their limited abilities to recreate the world of an English Renaissance drama, students may only succeed at producing worlds much closer to their own, Ostovich's approach nevertheless asks students to immerse themselves in a textual world, as is necessary for a formative use of literature, and it also gives opportunity for reflection on the worlds they manage to create through experiencing different groups' attempts.

Like Ostovich, Frances Teague, another of the contributors to this Approaches to Teaching volume, asks students to do much more than listen in her classroom. In her description of a particular instructional method she uses, she makes explicit her rationale for doing so. She's learned that academically skilled students who tend to take her course in Renaissance drama quickly become frustrated because the plays don't follow the character and plot development and the dramatic structure that they've learned to expect from Shakespeare and other later works. Rather than telling them outright to lay aside those preconceptions, Teague pushes them toward coming to that recognition themselves by assigning them weekly response papers in which they must address specific questions about the structure and characteristics of the play under consideration, questions to which these Renaissance dramas noticeably don't conform. What is the effect of this assignment? Teague writes,

> What I like best about the response papers, however, is the moment that arrives each term when the class revolts. About midway through the term, students begin to complain about the rigid questions. Why, they ask, must every play have a turning point or a protagonist or a genre? That moment exhilarates me, for they have learned on their own how conventional assumptions about drama can fail. The conversation that follows is always an exciting one . . . . In other words, the relative rigidity of the response papers leads students to question their own received wisdom about Renaissance drama.
>
> (69)

Some might argue that this method is both slow and labor-intensive, that it's far more efficient to tell students at the outset that these plays don't follow conventional assumptions, but with Teague's method, as she writes, "The key . . . is that that recognition originates with the students themselves rather than with their instructor" (71). Rather than being "merely witnesses" to the teacher's learning, here students are the agents of their own learning, thanks to an activity designed by their instructor. Teague effectively invites her students to participate themselves in scholarly work, learning through investigation the way that scholars do. Although the questions she asks students to address focus entirely on a critical-analytic approach to texts, her method potentially enables students to broaden their capacity to appropriate texts that don't fit the norms they've come to expect. This kind of mental expansion can assist students (or any readers) in their ability to recreate worlds from more remote texts. What students then do with this ability that Teague pushes them toward developing — whether they use it to help them recreate the text's world and then temporarily get lost in it — will depend on what else she asks of them in class.

Another intriguing instance of an instructional approach in which students take an active role is in Kathleen McCormick's description of the course she offers on *Ulysses*. During the semester, students will research and write "guides" to chapters of *Ulysses* that they've been assigned. These guides for each chapter — one student's focused on some aspect of the chapter's style, another on issues related to its production, and a third on its reception — are distributed to the rest of the students before they read the given chapter, and so these student-produced resources support the class's reading. Then the students who have written the guides give short presentations and facilitate the discussion of their chapter of *Ulysses*. While this method may appear to place the work of the course almost exclusively on students' shoulders, McCormick and the class's peer mentor, Melissa Shofner, emphasize the intense and at times exhausting effort required from them behind the scenes to ensure that the class is effective (387). An approach like this requires careful structuring and support, but the benefit is a class full of students who have wrestled at length with a portion of a difficult literary text and have become sufficiently expert in that portion to offer guidance and insight to one another. Whether *Ulysses* might then become a potential transitional object for students in a class like this is, of course, difficult to say, though learning how to make any sort of world from the words of a text like *Ulysses* certainly requires the kind of analysis involved in producing these guides. It does, however, become evident in McCormick's description that students also seemed to appropriate this text, to make it their own. The way in which her students took ownership of their own learning shows both an eagerness and an ease in their engagement with Joyce's work. McCormick writes, "Despite the fact that they were starting their final papers during the last few weeks of class, students continued to laugh easily, quote from *Ulysses* often, and, at the end of the semester, when I had left two weeks to workshop their final papers, they asked if we could start rereading *Ulysses* instead" (384). Though students' work in this class leans largely toward the reflective/distancing mode, this effort seems to produce a familiarity and an engagement that can foster the immersive experience of transitional space. Not only did these students take ownership of their learning, to some extent they took ownership of *Ulysses* as well.

McCormick's student-written guides and student-led discussions, Teague's use of response papers and Ostovich's student productions of Renaissance plays all illustrate methods of literature instruction that respond to the problems Blau and Scholes identify. In these instructional approaches, students acquire knowledge about the functioning of literary texts and the process of reading as they work through tasks or problems with which they are presented. Students become the learners rather than just the witnesses to the teacher's learning, and knowledge remains inseparable from its use. Classroom activities like those focused on Renaissance drama also highlight the contact with other cultures that literary reading makes possible. Teague's response papers draw attention to differences between contemporary assumptions about plot and those of Renaissance drama, while Ostovich's students must take on that remote culture as best they can in order to perform the plays. Literature classes that place students in active roles like these will foster in them a capacity to use texts as transitional objects when the tasks or problems students are given to work on require them to attend to the process of world-making that a literary text invites, like Scholes' discussion questions do or Ostovich's student-produced dramas. Space can then be made in the classroom for ways of reading that make possible the formative use of texts. Students have opportunity to see that literary reading involves making a world from a text and immersing oneself in it — even in school.

Yet what instructors ask of students in a literature classroom tends to be shaped by their notions about literary texts' role in society, at least in a number of the pedagogical texts I examined. To begin an exploration of a shift in conceptions of that role, and another trend within literary education conceived of as the students' activity, I want to return to Scholes' view of what it is that students need most from a "textual" education.

Literary education that prioritizes the ideological critique of texts

What students need more than the broad knowledge about a canon of literary texts that the coverage model offers, according to Scholes, is "textual power", which he defines broadly as "the kind of knowledge and skill that will enable them to make sense of their worlds, to determine their own interests, both individual and collective, to see through the manipulations of all sorts of texts in all sorts of media, and to express their own views in some appropriate manner" (*Textual Power*, 15–16). Instead of a "reverential attitude" toward texts, students need, in this "age of manipulation", according to Scholes, "a judicious attitude: scrupulous to understand, alert to probe for blind spots and hidden agendas, and, finally, critical, questioning, skeptical" (*Textual Power*, 16). An instructor's role then in what Scholes calls a "pedagogy of textual power", is to "help students to recognize the power texts have over them and assist the same students in obtaining a measure of control over textual processes, a share of textual power for themselves" (*Textual Power*, 39). Students begin to recognize texts' power and to retake some of that power through learning to practice the kind of criticism that "connects a particular verbal text with a larger cultural text" and its "systems of values" — with, in other words, "ideology" (*Textual Power*, 33). By beginning to identify the ways that texts shape culture and that culture shapes texts, students become less susceptible to texts' manipulations as they become more adept at recognizing how texts work in the world. While the importance is unquestionable of assisting students in gaining some mastery over texts that indeed can have power over them, I want to call attention to the apparently exclusive priority Scholes places on taking an attitude of suspicion toward texts in his conception of textual pedagogy, especially in light of the concerns of my previous chapter.

Although learning to resist texts' power seems to remain the ultimate objective in Scholes' instructional approach as he describes it in both *Textual Power* and *The Rise and Fall of English*, resistant or "critical" reading is not what Scholes asks of students initially, as the examples of his classroom discussion questions I mentioned earlier indicate. For Scholes, the process of reading that ends in a cultural or ideological criticism begins with an attitude closer to submission or receptivity toward the text. Scholes explains,

> Good reading involves reading every text sympathetically, trying to get inside it, to understand the intentionality behind its composition. It also involves reading every text unsympathetically, critically — but the sympathetic has to come first or the critical reading is impossible. If we impose our own values on every text, we have nothing to criticize but ourselves.
>
> (Textual Power, 169)

Scholes' description here of "sympathetic" reading resembles the immersive reading which is essential to the formative use of literature, yet, while the model of reading I presented in the previous chapter moves ideally (and in simplified form) from immersive reading through the critical or reflective and back to a form of immersion in the world of the text, Scholes' conception ends with the critical. Certainly there exist many literary texts whose worlds present such potential offense or harm for some readers that stopping at a critique would be well-advised, if not inevitable. Yet my concern in my reading of Scholes is for what may be excluded by his ultimate emphasis on enabling students to free themselves from the power of texts.

A recollection Scholes offers of his own literary education makes visible what is lost in the pedagogical approach he advocates, a loss he seems to consider unavoidable. Scholes uses the figure of Billy Phelps, who taught English at Yale from 1892 to 1933, to illustrate a conception of literature and literary education that he considers no longer viable. The general acceptance of universalism made credible the conviction that was "so obviously held by Phelps, that literature offered quasi-sacred texts that could be expounded by a licensed teacher/preacher to reveal the entrance to the kingdom of light" (*Rise and Fall*, 15). With the discrediting of universalism, this conception of texts could no longer be maintained and with it a role of literary reading that Scholes describes from his own past. He writes,

> When my professor of Romanticism told us how Wordsworth's poetry had comforted him in the trenches during the Great War, he was speaking, as he knew, to many of my classmates who had just come back from a greater one, but he spoke in the tradition of Billy Phelps, and his students still responded to that way of teaching. Nor am I about to claim exemption for myself from such sentiments, for I can remember only too clearly what it was like to sit in a convertible under a tree, mourning a lost love, and taking comfort from the poems of, yes Tennyson. Moreover, when I sailed off to defend "democracy" in Korea, I took a short anthology of poetry with me on the trip. My conviction that things have changed, then, is accompanied by a definite sense of loss, but I do not think nostalgia is a useful guide for action.
>
> (*Rise and Fall*, 13)

Here Scholes links the comfort he and his professor and classmates had taken from literary texts during trying periods of their lives with the view of literature as quasi-sacred texts. The implication of Scholes' treatment here of his past use of literary texts is that literature can no longer serve in such a role. For Scholes, literature's capacity to provide comfort in this way is unfortunately lost with its once-assumed ability to reveal universal truth. That Scholes' pedagogical approach ends with ideological criticism of texts is therefore a direct and intended outcome of the role he considers literature capable of fulfilling in society. The value for Scholes of teaching students to get inside a text, it seems, is primarily so that they can effectively critique that text, since he considers the possibility of taking comfort from literature to be a practice of the past that is no longer theoretically viable.

How is it, then, that literary study has value? Scholes writes, "If wisdom, or some less grandiose notion such as heightened awareness, is to be the end of our endeavors, we shall have to see it not as something transmitted from the text to the student but as something developed in the students by questioning the text" (*Textual Power*, 14). In other words, if the good of literary study can no longer be considered a result of the meanings a text conveys, then the only alternative Scholes sees is to locate its benefit in students' questioning of texts — in their judicious skepticism which enables them to exert a measure of their own power over texts. Although I in no way want to minimize the importance of enabling students to have some power over texts, all of which to varying degrees seek to manipulate their readers, I want nevertheless to stress that these claims Scholes makes suggest that for him the self-formational capacity of literary reading — a use of literature that can at times feel like comfort — is no longer credible because he considers it inextricably tied to a now-discredited universalism. The concept of the transitional object, however, provides an alternative foundation to this role for literary reading. Yet in a literary education that seeks ultimately to enable students to get out from under the power of texts, the capacity and opportunity to get lost temporarily in a text's world is neglected or even considered harmful, and so students' formative use of texts is challenged. Scholes' insights into the process of world-making in literary reading may still allow students to experience this kind of effect, but, if so, it would be merely incidental to the goal of his instructional approach.

A number of authors of other pedagogical texts share Scholes' conception of the objective of literary education, and they offer perspectives that can contribute to the question of the potential impact of conceptions of literature instruction on the formative use of texts. Gary Waller and the Carnegie Mellon English department he chaired in the late 1980s sought to teach students to use texts to read cultures. Published in 1996's *Critical Theory and the Teaching of Literature*, Waller's description of the theory-centered undergraduate English curriculum developed at Carnegie Mellon offers a compelling statement of the objective of this kind of course of study. Waller writes,

> Our goal is . . . to develop the skills and confidence (and some understanding of the epistemological underpinnings) to become strong readers of texts — "masterworks" and others — to be able to analyze the ideological dimensions of writing, of our own and others' readings, to raise questions of class, gender, race, and agency . . . In short, we are teaching our students not only a "subject" — English or literature — but also the ways through which they might know themselves as "subjects." Inseparable from the literary texts we read are the texts of our own histories, the text of the present, and the text of our historically and culturally constructed selves.
> (195)

Obvious in Waller's statements is the importance of the development of skills through a literary education as well as knowledge. The value of this learning and its potential use also reach far beyond the classroom and the field of study. Waller writes, "Whatever else we are doing in wrestling with developing curricular structures and pedagogical practices by which the new approaches can be introduced to students . . . we are helping students to make differences within their individual lives and, beyond that, to make informed interventions in the changes and chances of our society" (194). A literary education as conceptualized here seeks to help students learn how to identify the ways in which their culture shapes them and has shaped others, so that they might influence their society.

If courses taking such an approach invite and allow students to have their own readings of texts — to recreate the world of the text themselves — before inquiring into the ideological dimensions of both the texts and the varied readings students produce, this instructional approach could help students become more aware of factors which shape their experience of texts without first restricting the ways in which students read them. The student anthology and textbook of which Waller was an editor indicates that this is indeed what his approach allows. *The Lexington Introduction to Literature* calls on students to write "response statements" to the literary texts they read in which they are instructed to ask themselves three broad questions:

> How did you respond to the text?
> How did the text and you, as the reader, affect that response?
> What does your response tell you about yourself and your
> society? (15)

In asking first how students responded to the text, it is assumed that the student reader has produced her own reading of the text — allowing her to immerse herself in its world if she has already learned to do so — before she then steps back to examine her response to the experience and what in her and what in the text affected that response. Waller's colleague and collaborator, Kathleen McCormick, (who has recently written about her *Ulysses* course), more fully develops this kind of approach to literary education in *The Culture of Reading and the Teaching of English*, in which the readings students produce become the ground for the cultural or ideological analysis of both reader and text on which the course focuses. It is possible through these means that students might encounter for themselves the formational function of literary reading because the instructional approach does not seem to interfere with students' initial experiences of texts. Nevertheless, as in Scholes' conception of literary education, such an outcome would be incidental to the intended objectives of the approach.

Specific instructional methods are the focus of another essay on teaching literature as a form of cultural criticism. In a description of a particular course he teaches, Richard Miller of Rutgers University offers one conception of an instructional approach that asks students to connect "a particular verbal text with a larger cultural text", to borrow Scholes' phrase, an approach that is unusual in its focus and in the type of analysis it asks students to perform. Miller's course compares the ways a popular audience and a scholarly audience read a work of fiction, centered around Stephen King's *Misery*, a popular novel that, in the midst of the horror King is famous for, takes up questions of a popular writer's relationship to his audience and to the literary-critical establishment. Not only are students actively involved in thinking along with Miller in classroom activities, but, according to Miller's account, they are the ones who gather what becomes the content of the course. As I mentioned earlier in this chapter, Miller sends students outside the classroom to "research the ways the novel had been read", instructing them to ask questions like: "what makes certain ways of reading available to some readers and not to others? Which ways of reading the novel seem to predominate? How can one distinguish between a 'popular' reading of the novel and an 'academic' reading of it?" (132). Students then compile the various materials they gather into what they call the "reception database", which Miller describes in this way:

> The result of this effort to collect together, in 'inspectable form,' as much material evidence of actual instances of reception was a thick, ungainly, heterogenous 'book' that included among other things: interviews with King, reviews of the novel and the film from every conceivable mass-market magazine, articles about the popular book trade and the marketing of King's work, critical essays and excerpts from longer works examining the King 'canon,' and even a self-styled miniature ethnography cataloguing the reactions of family members, friends, and colleagues to the film adaptation of *Misery*.
>
> (133)

This "reception database" then becomes the resource students use for their own final projects. Miller explains how he asks students to undertake this final task and why he finds this approach worthwhile. He writes,

> One of the immediate benefits of having the students communally produce a text of this kind was that it meant there was no way I could claim mastery of the material they had collected. Indeed, the virtue of the database was that it provided all the students with a unique configuration of the novel's 'receptive' world, one that offered them the possibility of making original connections, of testing real hypotheses, and of genuinely assessing the merits of their own insights. From a certain perspective, then, the students were, in a limited but nonetheless real sense, 'free' in their final project for the course to make whatever they wished of the material.

They were simply instructed to "offer a reading of the [reception database] drawing attention to whatever [they found] most striking or significant about it, and articulating what 'story' — to borrow Geertz's term — that material has to tell about the culture that produced it."

(133)

In this course students gather the "data" themselves, analyze it, draw the conclusions that they see the data support, and produce as final projects their own contributions to the knowledge of the ways a popular literary text has been received. Because Miller as teacher cannot master the student-collected material of the course, he clearly becomes a learner along with the students who become experts on the subject to an extent themselves. If Miller's course is as successful in practice as it sounds in his written description of it, he has found an effective way to ensure that his students are the ones doing the learning in this course rather than merely observing their teacher's learning, and that the knowledge they acquire is both actively used and useful, at least as means of helping them understand the relations between a text and its cultures.

But what might be the implications of this instructional approach for students' capacity to make formative use of literary texts? What might students take from a course like this about ways that they themselves might read literature? (Though some might question the literariness of anything by Stephen King, there can be little question that a book like *Misery* could serve as a transitional object for some readers to some extent.) Miller's course does not primarily focus on assisting students with their ability to read fiction themselves, but provides them with the means and the motivation to research what others do with fiction (and with the film adaptations of fiction). Any potential impact, therefore, on students' capacity to use a work of fiction as a transitional object would emerge from the results of their research — what they learned from their inquiry into ways in which others have read a particular text and might therefore apply to their own reading practices, if they thought to do so. The outcomes of such an inquiry would be both fascinating and difficult to predict.

In these pedagogical writings of Scholes, Waller, and Miller, literary education as cultural or ideological critique leaves considerable uncertainty around the question of its effect on students' ability to have transformational encounters with literary texts. Students who arrive in courses like these with such literary encounters already well established in their past reading experiences may gain new insights and skills that broaden their understanding and appreciation of all that can take place between reader and text, and culture and text. The value of such learning should not be underestimated. If, however, some students have not yet experienced the potential of literary texts to serve as objects capable of provoking such formational experiences, their opportunity to encounter that possibility in a course in cultural criticism may be accidental at best. The focus of this type of approach to literary education lies elsewhere.

Two other iterations of a literary education as cultural criticism are worth mentioning, although they come from the context of secondary rather than post-secondary classrooms. While they provide helpful examples of ways to foster students' ability to question texts and ways of reading them, the specificity of their depiction of instructional methods makes visible some significant costs to students' literary encounters resulting from a narrow focus on reading critically. Bronwyn Mellor, Annette Patterson, and Marnie O'Neill represent the approach to literary education that became standard in Australian secondary classrooms. In their two books of readings and activities for students, they use a variety of means to raise students' awareness of how literary texts are constructed to make certain demands on readers and how readers bring culturally determined expectations to the texts they read. In one lesson, students are asked to predict what will happen in a short story before reading it, based on a brief description of the characters (a husband and wife and another younger woman who is their employee), to help them identify the cultural preconceptions of gender they bring to a text. After they've read the story, they compare their expectations to the story's events before reading another story taking a different approach to the same relational triad (*Reading Stories*, 1–23). In another instance, students are asked to write a story of their own, following a one-sentence synopsis of the story they will later read, a synopsis which for some students changes the protagonist's gender in order to make more apparent both the myriad choices an author makes in constructing a narrative and the role of gender in our interpretation and expectations of scenarios. After reading the published story, students compare it to the texts they wrote (*Reading Stories*, 45–54). And, in a third lesson, students are asked to consider two opposing perspectives on a story while reading it, a story which is apparently critical of racism. One view sees the story as an effective critique of racism, and the other sees hidden racist assumptions underlying the more explicit critique. Then they are asked to choose from lists of possible explanations for some of the actions in the story, explanations not explicit in the text, and to consider why the text doesn't fill in those gaps and what those gaps indicate about the story's assumptions about race (*Reading Fictions*, 66–70). These activities, of which I've only related the briefest of summaries, and the others in these two texts invite students' active engagement in the challenge of recognizing the many ways that culture shapes the ways we read and the ways we write, a recognition that's crucial if students are to learn to identify and resist gender, race, and class biases prevalent in texts.

But, as I asked of Richard Miller's approach, what will students learn about reading literary texts through the classroom activities Mellor, Patterson, and O'Neill construct? What conception of literature and its value will students take from a course like this? As Louise Rosenblatt observes, ". . . for some cultural, historical, or Marxist critics, texts became the complicitous indoctrinators of the dominant ideology. At best, it seemed, the reader could be taught to 'read against the grain' of the text in order 'to tease out' and resist its affirmation of the status quo" (*Reader*, 187). Likewise in this kind of literature classroom, students learn primarily that texts are "complicitous indoctrinators" that ought to be "read against the grain" so that their "affirmation of the status quo" might be resisted. While Mellor, Patterson, and O'Neill do include some texts in their books which themselves resist what might be considered the "dominant ideology", these texts are also treated as a focus for analysis from which students must "tease out" the assumptions they either affirm or challenge. Students are not given opportunity to engage with a text without explicit instruction that directs their attention only to issues of cultural bias. This instructional approach excludes from the classroom any recognition of the value of getting temporarily lost in the world of a text and any opportunity to do so.

The use Mellor, Patterson, and O'Neill make of texts in their instructional approach stems from their assumptions about texts: that "the starting point for any discussion about a piece of literature is the fact that it is a deliberate construction" produced and read in a particular cultural context, and that it carries assumptions and attitudes not all of which may be intended by the author (*Reading Stories*, xi). As their starting point, these concerns lead Mellor, Patterson, and O'Neill to make central to their pedagogical approach a "focus on the representation of gender, class, and race in literary texts" (*Reading Stories*, xi). While learning to see texts as cultural constructs is indeed an important part of becoming an astute consumer of media of all kinds, is that the best "starting point for any discussion about a piece of literature"? Literary texts certainly do perpetuate cultural assumptions, but that is not all that they do — that is not their only role. (If it was their only or even primary role, what would be the motivation, other than an act of political advocacy, to read a novel or short story outside of a classroom? And, even more, why would anyone ever write one?) Rather than fostering opportunities for contact with other cultures, Mellor, Patterson, and O'Neill's instructional approach is preoccupied with a critique of cultures. Motivated by their concern about the readings excluded or silenced by a culture's dominant ideology, this approach itself excludes other ways of reading literary texts, particularly the ways of reading that make self-formation possible.

The limited, antagonistic view of texts conveyed by Mellor, Patterson, and O'Neill's approach to literary education is not its only drawback.

Another concern their instructional methods make visible regards the roles implied for teacher and student. Pedagogical approaches that view students as active contributors to knowledge production tend to recognize the importance of establishing an atmosphere of open inquiry in the classroom, where the teacher's perspective, as well as the students', can be questioned. In this type of approach, Gary Waller claims that "the theories and theorizings of the teachers cannot remain immune from the same self-scrutiny that we wish our students to undergo in relation to their reading and writing experiences" (199). The objects of critique must extend beyond the texts and students' readings of them, and beyond the dominant ideology of a culture, to include the teacher's perspective as well. Mellor, Patterson, and O'Neill have come to the same realization, that they, as instructors, are not above ideological suspicion and that their viewpoints also require critique. They acknowledge as much directly to the students reading one of their textbooks when they write, "Like *all* the books you read, this book [*Reading Fictions*] is trying to *position* you to produce a particular reading. It argues that you should always ask how and why a text might be read in a particular way — and that includes this one" (*Reading Fictions*, 16). Although it offers students this invitation to question the perspective of the textbook, the instructional activities of this text make it extremely difficult for students to interrogate the perspective taken by their instructor (or, in this case, their textbook), and herein lies another difficulty of literary education as cultural or ideological criticism which Mellor, Patterson, and O'Neill's texts bring to light. The control they maintain over possible readings of the short stories they treat and the weightedness of the language by which they describe those readings leave little room for expressions of dissenting opinions or for questioning of the dominant perspective of their textbooks.

The activity which immediately precedes (and perhaps prompts) the declaration that this text "is trying to *position* you to produce a certain reading", makes apparent the normative nature of this literature classroom — where the teacher's perspective is constructed as obviously "right" and any other perspective as "wrong" or not worth consideration. Students are asked to read a story of a terrified woman alone in her apartment who senses the presence of an intruder, and then to read excerpts of reviews of the story from three unnamed critics. They are later asked to match each critic's reading of the story with one of the following descriptions.

Description A: This reading questions the sexist values that dominant readings of the text appear to support. Analysis of the ways in which particular readings are produced and what they might support is assumed to be important. It is argued that meaning is located not in the text but in the ways in which gender is constructed. Reading is thought of in social and political ways.

Description B: This reading supports dominant power relationships between women and men by not questioning them. Instead, the important issues of reading a text are located in questions of aesthetics — that is, how well a text is written. This approach has the effect of marginalizing other readings by simply not acknowledging the possibility that they even exist.

Description C: This reading acknowledges the possibility of other readings, especially feminist ones, but challenges them by claiming a kind of distance or objectivity, which the critic claims is authorized by the text. That is, the critic argues that this is the correct way to read the text. This is an attempt to marginalize or silence readings of gender issues as humorless and misguided.

(*Reading Fictions* 16)

According to these descriptions, one reading of the story "questions sexist values", while the other two "marginalize other readings" or "silence readings of gender issues". I expect that it would be obvious to most students that questioning, according to this textbook, is a "good" and marginalizing or silencing is a "bad", so that the question with which the lesson concludes would require little thought: "Can you decide which of the earlier critics' readings are supported by this book?" (*Reading Fictions*, 16). An instructional activity that draws differing perspectives in such stark terms does not leave students room for exploring alternatives, but instead marginalizes other readings itself, and not only sexist readings but any responses at all to the text that don't emphasize its gender bias.

Another activity in one of Mellor, Patterson, and O'Neill's textbooks asks students to characterize not a critic's reading of a short story but their own. In this lesson, students are given a brief summary of the story, including the surprising ending, followed by two different responses to that story or readings of it: that it's suspenseful entertainment or that it's "unacceptable and offensive". Students are then instructed to read the story and, during their reading, to record their agreement or disagreement with descriptions listed of these two different readings of the story, also a story of a woman alone with an intruder in her home. Descriptions of the first reading include: "has an engrossing plot", "has deft and amusing characterization", and "skillfully evokes the heroine's fear". Descriptions of the second reading include: "accepts and confirms that women may be victims of violence because of what they are — women", "implies women are silly to go out alone", and "implies women who are victims of violence are to blame in some way" (*Reading Stories*, 68). It seems hard to believe that any student going through this activity would feel free to check the "I agree" box after the statement that this story should be read as one that "skillfully evokes the heroine's fear", or the "I disagree" box after the statement that this story should not be read as implying that "women are silly to go out alone". Should some happen to choose counter to the position of the textbook, I would guess that the discussion following the activity would make clear to those students their error.

Through their textbooks Mellor, Patterson, and O'Neill do indeed work to "position" students "to produce certain readings", as they acknowledge, but in doing so their views maintain such dominance in the classroom that they are difficult to question and they appear to leave no room for any divergent perspectives. What might students learn from such an approach? To second-guess their own readings of texts and to depend upon the more authoritative (and correct) views of their teachers. To recall Deanne Bogdan's words, "While there is always somewhere to go in criticism, one can only be where one is" (148). By so assertively intervening in whatever readings students may have been able to produce themselves, these textbooks deny students the chance to "be" where they are — to read from the cultural positions or stances they occupy when they enter the class and from which they can then move to more self-aware positions. While an instructor like Waller may succeed in allowing his students to examine his position as a teacher (from positions of their own), his essay doesn't provide a description of instructional methods specific enough to offer evidence of his success or failure. Though Mellor, Patterson, and O'Neill express that same intention, the instructional activities they describe seem to make any such success an impossibility.

Deborah Appleman's *Critical Encounters in High School English*, another text focused on secondary literary education that I'm including in this discussion for the concerns it illuminates, offers yet another approach to literary education that involves cultural criticism. Appleman's approach introduces high school students to major schools of literary theory: reader response, Marxism, feminism, and deconstruction, and then asks them to read a literary text through each of those theoretical lenses, thereby developing in students the mental flexibility to take on other mindsets and an awareness of how different perspectives affect the way one reads. Like some of these other pedagogical texts, Appleman's expresses an interest in training students in skills that extend beyond reading literature, claiming that "contemporary literary theory provides a useful way for all students to read and interpret not only literary texts but their lives — both in and out of school" (2). Appleman's argument consists of not only a description of this approach and its rationale, but also a recounting of what occurred when she teamed with high school English teachers in taking their classes through the instructional activities she describes. It's in what occurred in those classrooms that my interest lies, because Appleman's account makes visible two other potential concerns about teaching literature as the practice of cultural or ideological critique.

Appleman's approach makes a needed intervention in a significant gap in much education, in which, as Appleman writes, "the biases that frame the particular perspectives of [students'] learning — whether scientific paradigms, historical school of thought, or approaches to literature — have never been admitted" (19). Students, she claims rightly, "need the tools that will help them recognize and evaluate the ideologies through which their education has been funneled" (19). This intervention, however, becomes problematic in a couple of ways. In teaching students, for instance, about deconstruction as a critical approach, Appleman provides them "with interpretive tools for critiquing the ideology that surrounds them", teaching them "to examine the very structure of the systems that oppress them and, in doing so, to intellectually dismantle them" (106). The object of students' early attempt at this intellectual dismantling in one classroom is John Donne's poem on the power of Christian resurrection, "Death Be Not Proud". A handout asks students "to contrast the author's intended meaning and the tools of traditional literary analysis with the consideration of how the poem might break down and work against the poet's intentions", and "to consider places where the text falls apart, where the threads of meaning begin to unravel" (107). However, the selection of students' deconstructive observations resulting from this assignment, offered as evidence of its effectiveness, exhibit more attitude than insight. I'll reproduce here the list of student observations Appleman selects in its entirety.

Why does he use the words "much pleasure"? He's trying too hard and we know it.

The poem breaks down when he offers that the only way to never have to face death is to die.

Do poppy and charms really make us sleep as well as death? Sorry. We're not convinced.

Death has power over us; it may be the only thing that does. He says "death shalt die" — but it never will die. He says "nor canst thou kill me;" but it can.

The poem is very contradictory. Donne attempts to dissect death and make it smaller, but the contradictions in the poem thwart the attempt and death ends up staying powerful and frightening.

First he asserts that a person can't die; then he describes how we do die.

He is trying to console himself, not the reader in this poem. I don't think he successfully manages to console either.

Though he says we wake eternally, he does not seem fully convinced that we do.

Although the poet is trying to convey that we must fight off death, that we are stronger than death, we, and he, cannot deny our fate.

The last line is completely indefensible. The punctuation also seems to add to confusion and may result in some unintended meaning.

(108)

Rather than critiquing any form of ideology or a breakdown in the poem's language, it seems that these observations show students attempting to "deconstruct" a poem they have not begun to understand, taking the sites of their own confusion as indications of the poem's "unraveling". Appleman inadvertently provides a dramatic demonstration of the importance of Scholes' claims that textual power requires reading sympathetically before reading critically and also that the skill of literary reading requires some knowledge, in this case knowledge of the Christian belief in resurrection. As these students' comments make apparent, any form of "critical" reading of a text that is not preceded by a sufficient "sympathetic" reading results in a critique of little more than a parody of that text. A danger, then, of cultural criticism as an approach to literary education at any level is that making critique the primary objective of reading a text can preclude learning to read that text at all, undermining any value in both the text itself and in the critique of it.

The other shortcoming of cultural criticism as an approach to literary education emerging from Appleman's pedagogical text is evident in one of the participating high school teacher's comments about the effects of this instructional approach. On a couple of occasions in her book, Appleman offers the reflections of classroom teacher, Martha Cosgrove. The following quote captures a noticeable movement in Cosgrove's thinking about Appleman's theory-driven approach.

> For me, teaching literary theory is about teaching kids metacognition and encouraging flexibility in thinking. It's about giving them power as learners, because literary theory enables them to know what they are doing while they are doing it. It's a bit like the Oz metaphor — lifting back the curtain and seeing the Wizard of Oz at work. And I feel very much like the wizard who exclaims, "Ignore that man behind the curtain!" One of the magical parts of teaching for me is creating circumstances for students which result in a magical act of understanding, of realization. When you give them the keys to even some of that magic, it is not magic anymore. (Unfortunately, this actually becomes a pretty big downside.)

(123)

For Cosgrove, the metacognition that is an objective of this instructional approach results in the diminishment of what she calls "magic". What does she mean by "magic"? She never offers an explanation, but in a statement Appleman includes later in her book, Cosgrove ties this magic with the reading of literary texts. Cosgrove says,

> So, kids are resistant to particular [theoretical] lenses for particular reasons. But are some resistant to lenses altogether? Probably the kids who don't want to analyze poetry to death. It's about breaking with the magic. And, as I've said before, I have very serious reservations about doing this. Those reservations seem more serious the more I think about them.
>
> (126)

Though Appleman includes in her book these two statements in which a teacher reports that she has "very serious reservations" about using this instructional approach, Appleman doesn't discuss these concerns, leaving us to wonder about them on our own. Why does Cosgrove say she has such serious reservations about teaching literature in this way? Implied in her statements is that analyzing poetry "to death", as a student might phrase it, means "breaking with the magic", something Cosgrove is resistant to do. "Magic", as a term, seems to be little more than grasping for a means to express a sense or an intuition of something missing in the outcomes of this instructional approach, a little-examined metaphorical expression. But the fuzziness of the term does not negate the importance of the statement and the phenomena to which it points. What might students learn about literary texts in a course on cultural criticism? Cosgrove implies that students learn that there is nothing "magical" about works of literature and the reading experiences they evoke. Some may consider the dispelling of this "magic" of texts to be a primary objective of their work as they strive to "free" students from the invisible domination of cultural objects like poems and novels. But Cosgrove feels that something valuable is lost in doing so.

With the insights of object relations theory, what Cosgrove calls the "magic" of reading literature can be understood as an attempt to articulate the powerful and indescribable experience of a literary work as an object in transitional space, when the boundary between self and text blurs and the reader is transported into a new world. Though the practice of ideological critique certainly plays a necessary role in our processing of the myriad texts we encounter, including literary ones, making such a practice the exclusive objective of a literary education can prevent students from experiencing literature's potential as transitional objects, at least in the context of school. Reading only for critique eliminates the opportunity for immersing oneself in a world. The "magic" of literature is then lost and, along with it, the vital reworking of self-other boundaries that literary reading can facilitate.

Though the approaches to literary education of Appleman and Mellor, Patterson, and O'Neill may not necessarily be representative of what is taking place in college literature classrooms, the concerns that their texts bring to light — in the midst of their contributions to a pedagogy of cultural criticism — can serve as valuable cautions for those who share their sense of the importance of the practice of ideological critique in the post-secondary context. First, when the ideological critique of texts is exclusively prioritized, the conception of all texts seem to be reduced to their role as vehicles for the propagation of cultural and ideological bias, leaving identification of that bias and resistance to it as the primary or even exclusive objectives of reading. Secondly, while claiming that all texts and all perspectives are open to questioning, instructional methods focused solely on critique can tend to convey to students that they are to accept uncritically and depend upon the more authoritative "critical" readings of their instructors and to second-guess the readings they themselves produce (if they in fact have learned to produce any). Thirdly, because of the predominance of the mode of critique in this approach, students may neglect or may never learn the careful reading practices that necessarily precede the effective critique of a text. And finally, and most significantly, when literary texts are considered only matter for ideological critique and if less antagonistic stances toward texts are not part of an education in literature, then ways of reading that make possible the use of literature as a transitional object — that evoke what might be called "magic" — are excluded from the educational context. Ideological critique of texts is a valuable practice for students to learn and should be an objective of a literary education, but when it is the only objective it can spoil the positive contribution literary texts can make in students' lives and in society as a whole. And it provides students little intrinsic motivation to read literary texts outside of school.

One other approach to literary education, and the last that I will discuss, seems to succeed at intentionally including in classroom activities the readings of texts that students initially produce as central to the focus of instruction, the very stage of textual interaction these other approaches can either overlook or work against.

Literary education that prioritizes students encounters with texts
In his 2003 book, *The Literature Workshop*, Sheridan Blau lays out an instructional approach that begins by inviting students to be where they are, to borrow again Bogdan's phrase — the place from which an ability to read literary texts can be built. For Blau, the goal of the classroom activities he devises "is to foster the development of a disciplined, autonomous literacy in students while building a culture of learning in the classroom that, unlike the prevailing culture of literary dependence and subservience, promotes the literary and intellectual enfranchisement of student readers" (34). Rather than teaching students to depend on others' more "expert" readings, as can inadvertently occur in other approaches where

teachers present their own readings either as the content of the course or as the more "critical" and therefore correct readings of literary texts, Blau designs classroom activities with the explicit objective of enabling students to read literary texts themselves.

To account for the importance of allowing students to work themselves at making some meaning from a literary text, Blau draws a distinction between the value of a reading and its authority. A student's early attempt at reading a poem, for instance, may have little authority compared to an expert's reading of that poem, but it will have value for her as a first attempt. Should that student repeat the interpretation of the poem that she heard from her instructor, that more proficient reading would certainly have more authority than her own early attempt, but it would lack value for her in her literary education because it was not something she had worked to acquire for herself. Blau illustrates the value of students' first and at times failed attempts to work out an understanding of a text when he recalls the student of his who lamented that his first reading of a poem for class was a complete waste of time. "That is," Blau writes, "he realized through his second and subsequent readings of the poem that his first reading was completely mistaken and took him in an entirely wrong direction in thinking about the poem" (197). The role of that misdirected first reading became apparent in class discussion when Blau asked the students if they couldn't be more efficient and skip the wasted first reading, moving directly to their second reading — or doing in their first time through a new text what they would usually do in their more productive second readings. Obviously such a feat is impossible, as any more successful subsequent reading depends upon the failed attempts that come before it. In literature classrooms that focus on instructors' or other experts' (or even students') "finished" readings of texts, this phenomenon will tend to remain hidden, likely leaving many students convinced that they are not capable of reading literary texts themselves because they cannot do in their first attempts what they see others like their instructors doing with texts.

Blau ensures that early confusion with a literary text maintains a primary place in his introductory literature courses by means of the first of the "literature workshops" in which he asks students to participate. According to his account of this workshop in his book's second chapter, Blau instructs students to read a selected poem three times, each time noticing whatever strikes them and rating their understanding on a scale of one to ten. After the third reading, students are to write about what they noticed happening to their understanding over the three readings and to write down any problems they still have with the poem. They then meet together in groups and talk about their reading, their understanding, and any questions they still have. After talking with the others, they are then asked to rate their understanding once more. Through these means students come to recognize literary reading as a process characterized by repeated (and sometimes failing) attempts at understanding, and one which requires effort and which also can benefit from taking the risk of discussing those attempts with others. This process stands in sharp contrast to the often-polished product students observe in teachers' and critics' pronouncements about a text. Additionally, this approach may allow issues of cultural difference, which are the concern of cultural criticism, to arise in these group discussions as students encounter differences in one another's readings, especially with the heterogeneity of many classrooms of students today.

Another of Blau's workshops emphasizes students' own experiences of a text while also allowing space for a diversity of readings of that text. It begins with an activity Blau calls "pointing". After reading a text once silently and then once aloud in class, usually a very brief short story in this case, Blau asks students to read out at random any line or phrase from the story that struck them as moving or memorable or resonated with them in any way, repeating lines as often as they choose. This unique way to "re-read" a text seems, Blau writes, "both to foster and to celebrate the reader's aesthetic experience of a literary work. It asks readers to re-create high points of their experience, not by talking about them, but by reliving those moments in the text in their own voices . . ." (146). This "re-creation" of the text not only allows students to experience again what moved them in their reading, but also allows them to experience what moved others, making visible and, in a way, share-able what is usually an individual and internal encounter with a text. And just as significantly, "pointing" allows students' classroom encounters with texts to be more than just critical or reflective by welcoming into the classroom a way of experiencing a text and sharing that experience that does not require talking *about* the text — that honors and in a way preserves students' immersive experiences of the text. At the same time, this activity can provoke the beginnings of reflection about differences in readings. Having sat in one of Blau's workshops myself, I remember being struck by a few of the lines that I heard read out, lines that seemed insignificant to me but that I then looked at differently because I heard that they were significant to other readers.

After hearing the text recreated in this way, students are then asked choose a line that they consider to be important to the text's meaning and very briefly to write about that line and why they chose it. They then share what they've written with a small group of students, noticing differences and similarities in how each other reads the story, before discussing what they've noticed together as a class. The cultural dimensions of the differences in readings that emerge as students share their perspectives can be tapped by asking students to follow their first written responses with a brief reflection on, in Blau's words, "how what they wrote in their response reveals something about who they are as 'situated readers', that is, as readers who occupy particular social roles in a particular cultural moment and setting (along with their roles in their own more personal and specific relational dramas)" (139). In this final phase of the workshop, then, students are asked to reflect on the possible sources of the readings they produced, having hopefully already recognized their own reading as one among many after hearing the differences in perspective among their classmates. Not only do students come to recognize the partiality of all readings through this workshop, just as cultural critics emphasize, but they also are allowed to develop a reading of their own — shaped as it may be by their own cultures — rather than primarily being asked to question the ways they and others read a text. Through an activity like this, the reading of a literary text can become a source of cultural contact, not only between the cultures of the text and of the reader, but also between the various cultures represented by the readers themselves.

The activity of "pointing" and writing about a line from the text can also allow or invite another approach toward texts, and one which Blau does not discuss in *The Literature Workshop*. In asking students to choose lines they find significant and to write about them, students may point out portions or aspects of the text that they find offensive or otherwise objectionable. While Blau's emphasis remains on viewing problems with a text as problems of the reader's understanding (an insight that may have helped Appleman's students in reading Donne), some difficulties that students identify through these means may persist. Through their discussion, students may in fact come to the conclusion that a text might provoke justifiable resistance — a stance toward texts that seems to be an instructional objective of literary education as cultural or ideological critique. However, through Blau's approach, the resistance would arise from students' reactions to their own reading rather than at the prompting of their instructor, although here the instructor's selection of texts, and general attitude and expectations would undoubtedly influence students' responses.

An approach to literary instruction like Blau's has the capacity to address the concerns of the cultural critic's approach as well as remedying some of its flaws. The activities that Blau has developed can enable students to recognize the variety of readings of a text that are possible and can give them opportunity to begin exploring the cultural sources of those readings as they interact with their classmates about their perspectives on a text. In this way this approach accomplishes one of cultural criticism's objectives, but in a manner that does not alienate students from their own readings nor construe texts as objects for critique only.

More significantly for my inquiry, this approach focuses initially on enabling students to have encounters with literary texts themselves. Though Blau's classroom activities do not especially emphasize the world-making quality of literary texts, nor the reader's opportunity to dwell in those worlds, they do foster in students the capacity to work through textual obstacles that might prevent them from being able to create a world from a text in their own reading. Then by inviting into the literature classroom pieces of students' literary experiences — re-enactments in a way of their "aesthetic" encounters with texts — this type of literary education makes space in the classroom for the immersive reading required by a formative use of literature, something that a cultural critique approach tends to neglect or even preclude. At the same time, however, Blau's approach lacks a justification of the importance of students' immersive encounters with texts, and, without a theoretically grounded conception of the value of this reading stance, its position can seem incidental and remains at risk.

So, remaining mindful of the inevitable discrepancies between writing about teaching and what actually transpires in classrooms, what can we surmise may be the potential effects of recent approaches to literary education on students' capacity to use literary texts as objects in transitional space? When instruction is considered to be primarily the instructor's activity, student learning is difficult to determine as the appropriation of whatever the instructor asserts or models is left up to the ingenuity and resourcefulness of the students themselves. The focus of the instructor's activity, in its typical emphasis on more critical treatments of texts, will tend to shape students' conception of literary reading, often to the exclusion of the immersive reading mode that gives the critical its meaning. When students play an active part in instructional activities, the likelihood that they are learning increases as they become co-producers of the content of the course rather than just observers of their teachers' efforts. But the effect of that learning on their capacity to make formative use of literary texts depends upon what they are asked to do with literature. If students are not invited and enabled to produce their own readings of texts or if the readings they are asked to produce prioritize a critical or resistant stance toward texts, their literary education will at best marginalize their formative literary encounters if it doesn't obstruct them or even prevent them entirely. A number of these pedagogical texts emphasize the importance of fostering students' experiences of engagement with works of literature, but none of these offers an articulation of the significance of such engagement as substantial as the self-formational capacity of transitional objects. With the insights of object relations theory, the aesthetic engagement that some of these teachers of literature value and that others consider passé becomes justifiably the very heart of the matter of literary reading, and an instrumental heart at that. But this heart of the matter faces an additional and unavoidable challenge in the context of education that calls for a brief discussion before I conclude this chapter. That challenge is the culture of schooling.

The Challenge of the School Context

The tension between literary reading and school expectations was obvious in the remarks of Jeffrey Wilhelm's avid middle school readers about the differences between their reading experiences in school and out of school, as I related in the previous chapter. While these students read enthusiastically and in some cases incessantly on their own time, they did not consider the literary reading expected of them in school to be at all engaging or personally satisfying. They saw school reading as reduced to a matter of correctly answering the questions at the end of a text. It seems they are not alone in that experience, as this perception is something I hear often from my own students, and so I think it worthwhile in this inquiry to articulate some concerns about this conflict as it will necessarily affect what can be accomplished in a school context regarding literary reading.

As I mentioned at the outset of this chapter, Marshall, Smagorinsky, and Smith's study of secondary literature classes disclosed a gap between teachers' intentions for their students' interactions with literary texts and what students actually do in their classrooms. While students in classroom discussions displayed little of the engagement, initiative, and meaningful interaction with literary texts their teachers hoped to see, these researchers, in another of their studies, did observe this kind of involvement in students' discussions of literature outside the classroom. In informal interviews with adolescent readers outside of the school context, students' responses to literary texts had a more personal or moral dimension, though in language outside the norm for academic literary analysis (126). Out of the classroom, in language of their own, students did produce readings of literary texts that held personal meaning for them. From these studies, Marshall, Smagorinsky, and Smith conclude that

> . . . conventional patterns of discourse in classroom discussions are *not* inevitable; . . . they only *seem* right and proper because of their ubiquity. But the salience of traditional patterns of discussion makes it easy for teachers to fall back into them even when they are working to change. Further, because the speech genre of classroom discussions of literature had conditioned the ways that students think about litera-ture even when teachers invite them to respond in new and different ways, students might refuse or fail to recognize those invitations . . .
>
> (131, italics original)

In other words, while students may be capable of meaningful engagement with literary texts outside of school, teachers' efforts to enact approaches to literary education conducive to such engagement may be thwarted by the environment of schooling itself, characterized by the familiar instruc-tional patterns to which teachers tend to return when faced with students who continue to exhibit the habits instilled in them by years of school.

Changing instructional patterns requires not only changing the teacher's own habits but the students' expectations as well.

English educator Alan Purves acknowledges the influence of readers' schooling on their expectations of reading and reading instruction. Based on years of research into readers in school, according to Purves, " . . . we know that readers are not naïve," but they bring into the classroom with them what is "in great part the product of the culture of school literature that inculcates ways of reading texts and talking about them" (349). By the time a student arrives in a post-secondary literature class, he carries already-established habits and expectations for what the school context will require of him regarding a literary text, shaped by his previous school experiences. Some students, like Wilhelm's avid readers, have learned to separate their personal literary experiences from those they have in school, giving free reign to the former while restricting their expectations for the latter. Others seem never to allow their encounters with texts to escape the narrow conception of literary reading they may have derived from the testing and worksheets of many primary and secondary schooling settings. Whatever students' expectations, an instructor must reckon with them because they will certainly influence how students take up the tasks asked of them in a new classroom.

Why do these schooling habits, which both students and teachers have acquired, often tend to produce so unfavorable an environment for literary reading? The need for testing and grading, and the conformity these practices promote are surely primary contributors. But so are the very logistics of school. In remarks that I think are as valid for the educational setting today as they were when they were published several decades ago, Walter Slatoff powerfully captures this aspect of the conflict between the realities of school — whether secondary or post-secondary — and the reading of literary texts. He claims that the total environment in which we teach literature helps to prevent the fullest experience of literary texts. To illustrate why, Slatoff asks us to imagine

> . . . a student sitting at a desk in a row of desks at 9:44 on a Tuesday morning with the class to end in six minutes, at which time he will have to rush to physical education or psychology class, trying to consider seriously the meaning of the lines "Ripeness is all" or "In every voice, in every ban, / the mind-forg'd manacles I hear". He has to hold himself reasonably aloof; he has to respond with only a small and temporary part of himself or he might well forget to copy the next day's assignment or to get to his next class. He might weep or exclaim. He might quit school altogether for a week. He might, after reading a poem about the desperate loneliness of all people, take hold of his neighbor's hand.

(175–76)

As Slatoff describes, the effects of literary reading don't fit into the scheduling and decorum required in school, not to mention the requirements of a manageable curriculum and a means of assessment. In the face of this sharp incongruity, it's easier if literature in the curriculum and classroom "becomes essentially subject matter to be studied and talked about like other subjects and other matter" (176). To accommodate the demands of schooling, the ways of reading literary texts that allow their formative use can be neglected. Seeking to change this phenomenon requires addressing long-established habits and expectations that have been shaped by the logistical limitations and requirements of the school context.

My intent in this chapter has been to examine how various approaches to literary education can limit students' opportunity to use works of literature as transitional objects, along with the challenges presented to this use by the schooling environment. In the next and final chapter of this project, I will endeavor to make explicit some specific considerations by which this capacity might be more intentionally welcomed into post-secondary literary education.

4 Toward a Literary Education Conducive to the Formative Use of Literature

As I approach the end of this project, it may be beneficial to recall where I began. The question: Why literature?, which motivates this study, emerged as I sought to translate my own instructional approach from the composition classroom to the literature classroom. In teaching composition, I work to construct a classroom situation in which the students and I are co-inquirers together focused on the broad objective of defining and producing effective written communication, while also creating opportunities for students to experience the value of writing effectively through reading one another's written work and hearing others' responses to their own. While the objective of composition instruction seems clear to me, and its value evident both in the academic context and in life beyond schooling, articulating the objective of a literary education is more problematic. To say simply that a literature course should enable students to read literary texts leaves unanswered the crucial question of the value of such "reading" (as well as the question of what such reading entails). What should a literature course seek to make possible for students and for what good? The lack of a widely accepted conception of the value of literary reading has been a well-acknowledged gap in the profession as a whole. I've argued that this need has undermined the effectiveness of literary education, a possible factor in the tenuous role of literature in society at present.

While many acknowledge that literature provides enthralling and even transformative experiences for many readers, understanding the reading of literature as a transitional object in Winnicott's terms means that such reading experiences are actually as vital for human functioning as they often feel for avid readers. Through the mechanism of transitional space, the temporary blurring of boundaries that occurs in immersive reading facilitates a reworking of the self's relations across those boundaries. This in-between space allows us access to otherwise unavailable parts of ourselves, makes possible the readjustment of the boundary between self and other, and gives us opportunity to try on new ways of being in the world, effects which can reverberate through cultures as well as in individuals. So, if literature can serve such an important formative human function, what does that mean for literary education, for how we teach this subject? It means that one of the central objectives of literature instruction should be ensuring that students have opportunity to use literary texts in this way — to immerse themselves in the world of a text, making the shapes of that world available for the working out of their selves in their worlds through the temporary blurring of boundaries between inner and outer experience. Undoubtedly, literary reading offers other contributions to learning, including a form of historical knowledge and occasions for the development of skills in textual criticism, but what sets literature apart from other types of texts is its particular capacity for inviting the psychological and cultural work that transitional space makes possible. Facilitating that use should therefore form the heart of a literary education.

Here at the conclusion of this project I want to propose some principles and a few ideas for practice that can make literature instruction more conducive to formative experience, but I do so with a measure of reserve. In an article in *College English*, Don Bialostosky offers the journal itself some advice, and his counsel is equally appropriate for this work as well. He urges the journal "to cultivate patience in its contributors, soliciting their articulation and evaluation of pedagogies without insisting that their articles end with hastily cobbled-together alternatives to the erroneous views they have exposed or jerry-rigged solutions to the problems they have uncovered", adding that problems critiqued can be "so widespread and deeply embedded that the solutions might need the work of many colleagues over some time to address them" (115). Likewise with my project, recommendations for instruction emerging from this inquiry are only preliminary and provisional. I am, at this writing, little more than a few years into working out these ideas in college literature classrooms. A thorough exploration of ways this formative view of literary reading might influence or contribute to literature education will involve many more years than those I've yet invested in the process, but doing so is indispensable. Putting ideas about education into practice is essential, as Martin Bickman observes, "if they are to be made viable and complete". He continues, "Only by enacting them can we see their full implications and begin to further clarify them" (151). As I continue to enact these ideas and experiment as a teacher, my thinking continues to evolve. What I am ultimately proposing here for the field of literary studies is an alternative sense of direction and rationale for its pedagogy, and, through offering my ideas for practice in their present form, I hope to invite others to think along with me about ways in which literature instruction might better facilitate formative experiences with texts. Miriam Marty Clark is one who has recently begun such work on teaching methods in her article, "Beyond Critical Thinking", where she explores ways of teaching literature for appreciation rather than mainly for critique. To efforts like hers, my project contributes a more developed justification and objective. So it is in a spirit of expectancy for future collaboration that I offer the pedagogical implications to which this inquiry has led me thus far.

Principles for Instruction

Because formative work is largely unconscious, it cannot be directly taught, as I've claimed. Any psychological effect of a literary work can be difficult if not impossible to predict or to orchestrate, as it occurs on the occasion of a seemingly uncanny resonance between a particular text and an individual reader (shaped though she is by the broader culture which she inhabits). The triggers for such influential reading encounters are usually beyond the awareness of even the reader in whom they occur. It would therefore be unrealistic for an instructor to expect to be able to provoke in most of the students in a class a formative experience with even a few of the literary works she assigns. Rather, she can at best endeavor to both invite and facilitate immersive reading as the mode essential for transitional space, and attempt to avoid obstructing or impeding potential experiences in this in-between space by over-determining what students do in their encounters with texts. While students cannot be taught how to use literature as a transitional object, their capacity to make such use of it can be spoiled by the expectations and requirements of a literary education. Instruction can best foster the formative capacity of literary reading when it provides opportunities for students to engage with texts in such a way that they might become for them objects in transitional space, and when it works to remove obstacles that would prevent such engagement. The recommendations that follow describe an instructional approach with this purpose.

The priority of immersion in a text

For the reader's experience of the text's world to be available as an object in transitional space, as I've said, the reader must immerse himself in that world. For literary education this means that an immersive stance toward texts must not only be made visible in instruction but must take priority, not to the exclusion of the reflective, distancing mode of reading but as the context or frame in which the latter gains its significance. This shift in priority is called for when students both initially and finally engage with literary texts, if, as Ricoeur suggests, interpretation begins with a naïve, immersive mode, proceeds into critical or distancing reflection, and then returns to an immersive stage. Students first need to be allowed to have their own initial "naïve" reading of a text and to attend to that experience as a part of the subject matter of the course. To invite them, for instance, to write and then talk about what the world they have recreated in their reading looks like and feels like from within it will help them recognize that temporarily dwelling in an imagined world is what literary reading makes possible and what forms its substance, as it also furthers their understanding of what that process involves and how it differs for different individuals. The analysis and critique, which have typically been the preoccupation of college-level literature instruction, take on significance for students then as means of exploring or resolving questions and objections that arose in their encounters with the literary work. Informed by that analysis, students can then return to an immersive stance if given occasion to put themselves into the world of a text again, this time able more fully to appropriate the text — to inhabit it or to make it a part of themselves. Literature instruction for formative reading thus prioritizes immersion in a literary world rather than the more customary critical detachment as the culmination of a course as well as at its outset.[1]

Beginning with students' experience of texts

Immersive reading depends upon an even more fundamental occurrence, one that may sound too obvious to mention. If students are to be able to immerse themselves in literary worlds, then they themselves must read or, more accurately, experience the text.[2] The textual world in which a reader temporarily loses or releases her clearly bounded sense of herself must be the world which *she* recreates in interaction with the text. If she depends primarily on the readings of her instructor, published critics, or anyone else, she will lack her own experience of the text which is the location of any potential formative work. This is the first of a number of the claims at which I've arrived at the conclusion of this inquiry that find a strong resonance in writings of Louise Rosenblatt.[3] Decades ago she made a similar claim in recognizing that a literary text is nothing more than marks on paper until it is read. It becomes, in her words, the "poem" or the literary work only as the reader calls it forth — only in what he experiences himself

---

1 In a departure from Ricoeur's thought, I am advocating this positive mode of appropriation as the final stance toward texts not because there is some transcendent "meaning" to be restored as Ricoeur contends, but to make the text available as a "transitional object" for readers' psychic use.

2 This is not to exclude hearing a text read aloud, as is the primary literary experience of many children who become readers of literature, but to emphasize that students must have their own experience of a text whether or not they themselves are decoding the words on the page.

3 The approach to literary instruction I advocate shares much in common with Rosenblatt's (which is more sophisticated than the simplistic, culturally naïve Reader Response approach that tends to be attributed to her). What my project ultimately contributes to Rosenblatt's pedagogical work is a honing of focus and a theoretical justification both provided by an understanding of the value of reading literature that is informed by the concept of transitional space with its role in psychological and social self-formation.

in relation to the text. In Rosenblatt's memorable comparison, "Accepting an account of someone else's reading or experience of a poem is analogous to seeking nourishment through having someone else eat your dinner for you and recite the menu" (*Reader*, 86). A literary education centered on the formative use of literature must first allow and enable students to read literary texts themselves or, more specifically, to construct from a text a world. Then that textual world can become a potential transitional object as a reader allows himself to temporarily inhabit it.

With some works of fiction constructing a world from the words on the page may appear effortless for many readers. The passionate attachment many thousands have experienced with the Harry Potter series, for instance, suggests that recreating its world happened easily for most who picked up these books. This is not likely the case with many literary works assigned in college classrooms however. Whether it's Joyce's *Ulysses* or Homer's *Odyssey*, most students' initial "naïve" reading may produce far more confusion or even boredom than an experience of an imaginary world into which they can immerse themselves. A work's complexity or its cultural distance from students prevent many a text from offering especially less-prepared students much more than an initial confounding experience, but that experience — whatever characterizes it — is still the ground from which students' literary education arises. What takes place in the classroom should be largely shaped by the experiences the students are having in their encounters with the text if it is to build on their abilities to read literature themselves.

But beyond their importance in keeping classroom work relevant, students' experiences with the texts of a course should also be of keen interest to teachers and scholars concerned with what transpires between literary texts and actual readers, rather than just ideal or otherwise generalized readers who tend to be the focus of many Reader Response theorists. This is why Bickman considers the classroom to be "the best laboratory, the most dependable source of data" about actual readers (153). The written work and discussion of a class can make visible the practices, obstacles, and effects of real readers encountering particular literary works. While focusing initially on students' experiences with a text does offer a sort of scholarly data, it is ultimately of central importance as the location of any potential transitional activity. Often, however, those initial reading experiences fail to make from the words a world or even much meaning at all. Then the distancing stance of analysis takes on one of its valued roles as means toward remedying that failure.

Reflection and analysis in a supporting role
In a literary education for the formative use of literature, reflective or distancing reading serves immersive reading in this and a couple of other essential supporting roles. As I've learned from my own "quick" and

unsatisfying reads of *Moby Dick* and *To the Lighthouse*, the complexity of many literary works will to varying extents exceed readers' capacity to construct a world except with much reflection and re-reading. Stepping back from the text to acquire some knowledge about it is often necessary to recreate its world, especially for those texts that frustrate students' expectations. That knowledge — whether it is some historical context or the role of a particular stylistic device — becomes instantly both useful and used when it addresses a problem students have already experienced with a text. While key information can be effectively provided through lectures, students can also be prompted to perform their own inquiries, drawing on outside sources or focused investigations into the literary work itself. When I read *Ulysses* as an undergraduate, it was at best a perplexing curiosity until I was asked to write a paper on the two occasions in the work when Joyce uses the word *omphalos*. My own inquiry into the word (Greek for *navel*) and its importance in Joyce's work yielded for me such meaningful insight that it transformed my sense of the text as a whole. The exercise permanently influenced my conception of what approaches are worth taking with literature. Although it's a rather extreme example, my experience with *Ulysses* demonstrates the crucial role of reflective or distancing reading as it makes possible immersive reading by assisting readers in more fully evoking a world from the work. Much of the content of literature courses, if the MLA's Approaches to Teaching series is any indication, gains value for students primarily in the context of this broader objective, as means to assist students in more fully apprehending the literary work.

A second role for reflective or distancing reading emerges from readers' interactions with the world of a text. As they are asked to recreate and immerse themselves in textual worlds, particular students may likely resist particular texts or aspects of them. Depending on their own situation, feeling state, or ideology, students will at some point in their reading step back from a text and say "I object —" as I did myself, for instance, at my reading of William Styron's *The Confessions of Nat Turner*. That a white male author should portray the black male hero of his novel (and an important historical figure at that) as irrationally and almost debilitatingly obsessed with a young white girl seemed to me unfair and even harmful in its presumption. As a result of my response to Styron's depiction of Turner, I read much of the novel with considerable suspicion and mistrust, keeping myself at a distance from its world. The possibility of such resistance is an important part of a reader's interaction with a text, as students need to be helped to take back some textual power for themselves, to borrow Robert Scholes's phrase. It should therefore be a valued part of a literature classroom, with a couple of important conditions. First, readers' resistance to a work of literature, especially student readers, can often be more a factor of their misunderstanding of the text than of a problem within the text itself, as in my discussion in the previous chapter of Appleman's high school critics of a Donne poem. (It's important, though, to acknowledge that one cannot definitively distinguish between a textual problem and a problem of the reader's understanding.)[4] Students need to be pushed initially to question their own resistance, to give a text the benefit of the doubt and to work at working out a more generous understanding of the text, in order to avoid rejecting what they haven't begun to understand. Secondly, because it's essential in this approach to literature instruction that students themselves read texts rather than depending on others' readings, any resistance to a text should arise from students. When students are invited to bring into the classroom what they have made of a literary text — their experience of its world as they've reconstructed it — the resistance that may have characterized the readings of some becomes part of the matter of the course, available for the reflection of all and a potential source of the learning about texts and experience of texts for all the students in the class. Should such resistance be an intended focus of a course, the instructor can ensure that it will arise in students' reading by choosing texts likely to provoke it.

This interaction of a classroom community of varied readers facilitates a third role for reflective distance in literary reading: reflecting on the reading process itself — the way literature works on readers and readers work on literature. While an individual reader can come to some measure of awareness of her own interaction with a text by standing back, so to speak, to consider what she has done and what has been its outcome or effect, the distance required for such reflection can be more fruitfully produced by hearing from others what they have done with a text. Difference breeds awareness as it draws attention to what might otherwise remain implicit. I will never forget the class member who read as humorous a short story others read as tragic, or the student who saw a life-affirming ending to a story where most in the class read grief and loss. My surprise at these very different readings pushed me back to the text and prompted me to question both the text and us as readers — what in our past or makeup inclined us to see these texts in such widely divergent ways. The discovery of differences can indeed provoke investigation into factors contributing to them whether cultural or personal, and the participants' awareness or understanding of both self and others increases, as does their knowledge of what literary reading involves. Other than a book club or reading group, the literature classroom is a rare occasion where the internal, individual process and

---

4 This is a problem Sheridan Blau addresses at length in the ninth chapter of *The Literature Workshop*.

experience of literary reading can be shared.[5] The nature of the world a reader recreates from a literary text and her experience of it reveal much about that reader as well as about the process of literary reading more generally. When student readers are invited to bring into the classroom their experiences of texts, their reflection on those experiences can serve as an almost limitless source of learning.

The role of students' reflection on their literary encounters does raise a question for this study. Because the formative use of literature or any other object is generally an unconscious process, readers, of course, need not be aware of this psychic function in order to benefit from it. Is it then helpful in a literary education conducive to the formative use of literature that students be explicitly introduced to this aspect of psychoanalytic theory, that they become mindful of its operation? While, of course, an individual need not know about transitional space for it to function, it may be beneficial for students, based on my own experience of the impact of acquiring a conception of transitional objects and their use. This concept has provided me with an explanation for the power or attraction of certain objects or pastimes for certain individuals — why, for instance, a particular song will feel so deeply satisfying for a time that I'll listen to it over and over or why the world of *The Brothers Karamazov* during my hurried reading of the novel for a class seemed more real than my own world and left me feeling changed as I attempted to re-enter ordinary life. Even more significant than gaining this understanding, though, has been gaining a sense of the importance of these experiences — the choices that may tend to be discounted as just a matter of personal preference in actuality serve a vital psychological function. Gaining an awareness of the use of transitional objects has enabled me to recognize the value of preferences that could otherwise seem insignificant, and it can do the same for our students. This awareness has more than a personal significance too. The conception of the use of transitional objects has the potential to provide a rationale for the arts as a whole that is sorely needed in our society. For

---

5 This potential of literary education is yet another insight Rosenblatt recognized. In her words,

> The reader, reflecting on the world of the poem or play or novel as he conceived it and on his responses to that world, can achieve a certain self-awareness, a certain perspective on his own preoccupations, his own system of values.
>
> Learning what others have made of a text can greatly increase such insight into one's own relationship with it . . .. Through such interchange he can discover how people bringing different temperaments, different literary and life experiences, to the text have engaged in very different transactions with it.

(*Reader*, 146)

these reasons, this formative use of literature and other objects or pastimes is worth introducing explicitly to students.

While reflection on the practice of literary reading is essential to establishing a conception of its value, the heart of the matter in this approach to literary education is still students' experience of immersing themselves in the world of a text, a world which they themselves have recreated. Distancing themselves from the text can assist them in more fully recreating that world, can allow them to assert themselves against a text, and can enable them to gain greater awareness of the process of literary reading and its value. But it is their experience of getting lost in the text's world that makes possible their own encounters with the formative effect of transitional space.

That said, in my own teaching experience of the last few years, many of my students did not get swept up in any text's world in my classes, even with the freedom to do so and the support of reflection and analysis toward that end. Why? Due to my course assignments most of the literary works I've taught recently have been at least four hundred years removed from students, a challenging gap for many to cross. The struggles students have with texts from long ago and far away foreground the role of culture in literary reading. Though many were unable to immerse themselves in the literary worlds of Homer or Dante, attempting to do so provides an especially effective occasion for building cultural awareness.

Attending to culture

Certainly literary works that are far removed from readers' cultural locations can still provide formative experiences when even a small portion of a text offers the needed resonance with a reader. For instance, the depiction of Gilgamesh's cry of desperation as he walks for days through a dark tunnel catches my breath when I merely recall it, as I do from time to time. That the image has become a sort of fixture in my imagination suggests that it plays a formative role for me. Yet when such resonance is lacking, the process of attempting to "live into" a literary work, to borrow Gary Saul Morson's phrase (355), still carries significance as readers attend to the experience. To recall Gabriele Schwab's observation (which I discussed in Chapter 1), it is when we face a thoroughly foreign text or a radically different style that we are reminded that reading "always requires a certain negotiation of otherness, a mediation between two more or less different cultural or historical contexts, the text's and the reader's" (*Mirror*, 9). Encounters with texts that are culturally distant bring that negotiation of otherness into the foreground, but only when students are prompted to see it as such.

That some students puzzle over why the *Aeneid* tells us the end of its story in its opening lines points to a cultural difference in the expectations for stories and their function that's worth exploring. Similarly, that many students find the stylized, formal language of the poetry of Renaissance England off-putting demonstrates a difference not only in expectations, but in what is valued between that time and this. A text only decades older than my students, but still culturally removed from most of them, can also present challenges. The student of mine who found the characters' names in Toni Morrison's *Song of Solomon* to be ridiculous (names like Guitar, First Corinthians, and Milkman) was ready to dismiss the entire novel as too far-fetched to be in any way believable, but his frustration suggested that he was experiencing a clash of cultural assumptions. Instead of rejecting the text for its ridiculous names, I urged him (not quite successfully) to ask what this way of giving and receiving names might suggest about the world of Morrison's novel and the racial relations it portrays. A further question worth considering is what his own assumptions about naming, brought to light by the apparent strangeness of the text's assumptions, suggests about his own world. An essential part of an instructor's task is to push students toward recognizing that what may frustrate, confuse, or even bore them in reading a text may be a form of cultural contact, an experience of difference worthy of reflection.

An approach to literature instruction that prioritizes both immersive reading and students' experiences in attempting such reading invites conflicts like these to become a part of the matter of the course, enabling students to become more aware of the role their own cultural locations play in their encounters with literature and the negotiation that reading involves. I'm convinced that many if not most of the difficulties students have with literary works arise from cultural differences as even the formal qualities of a text are manifestations of the culture from which it emerged, and students' expectations for different types of texts are shaped by the cultures they inhabit and the genres to which they are accustomed. In a discussion in my ancient world literature course, I learned that a number of students considered Odysseus unheroic because he is unfaithful to his wife, he often weeps openly, and he does little without Athena's help, behaviors not appropriate for a hero, according to these students. These objections gave form to the cultural conflict students were experiencing with the world of *The Odyssey*, and they gave focus to our class inquiry into differences between Odysseus' culture and ours, differences in conceptions of a hero, expectations of marriage, expression of emotion, and the relationship between humans and the divine.

To guide students in the literary encounters of a course, I've adapted Gayatri Spivak's formula for reading. She instructs students in her graduate courses not to excuse the text, nor to accuse the text, but to use the text by entering into its "protocol". In the context of a literature course, I deemphasize the "use" of a text in order to focus primarily on the experience of attempting to enter its "protocol", to insert oneself into its world on its own terms rather than on ours. For example, rather than ignoring or overlooking Odysseus' marital infidelity on one hand or, on the other, dismissing the work as worthless or even harmful because it is obviously sexist according to today's standards, reading *The Odyssey* on its own terms means acknowledging that Odysseus seems to suffer for his arrogance but not for having sex with women (or goddesses) other than his wife. Condemnation for that act is not part of the protocol of the text. Reading in this way requires a temporary suspension of one's own values and expectations in order to take on, as best one can, the perspective of the text itself, to attend to the values of its world and to place oneself within it in order to see what one can see from that other position. Then, with the benefit of that alternative view, one returns to one's own perspective, perhaps to critique the text's world or one's own, having temporarily seen through other eyes. To place Morson's phrase into the sentence from which it came, "Great works invite us to do two things: first, 'live into' them and understand them from within; then, enter into dialogue with their perspective from one's own" (355). Here again, with a slightly different slant, is the cycle of an immersive movement into the text followed by stepping back from the work that has come up repeatedly in this inquiry. An understanding of transitional objects endows the "living into" mode with even greater potential, as this encounter with another culture can leave its imprint on the reader through the permeability of that in-between space.[6]

Whether these students' experiences reading *The Odyssey* could be considered to occur in transitional space, I cannot be sure, but it is clear in the written reflections of many of them that their experience influenced their ways of negotiating the boundary between self and other. Meagan O'Reilly's observations about what she gained as a student in the ancient world literature course I taught convey especially well what others claim to have noticed as well. She writes,

Through the readings and discussions in this class I found that it was important to release myself from the standards of social convention and the ideals of my cultural experience before reading. This makes the interaction between myself and the text more gentle; I am not constantly scrambling to make sense of the text from my narrow experience of the world and the text does not suffer the manipulations this judgment would necessitate . . . . the practice of letting go of certain assumptions about the world when coming into contact with a different perspective, in order to understand what I am presented

---

6 It's important to acknowledge the possibility that the imprint left on the reader may not actually be beneficial. This is a matter I hope to take up in a later project.

with, has taught me to allow a pause of consideration instead of immediately passing judgment. I believe this is the basis of tolerance and healthy human relationships.

O'Reilly's reflection on the process of reading a text culturally distant from her demonstrates how immersive reading can affect relations across difference in a conscious and intentional way as well as through accessing transitional space.

This broad conception of a literary education conducive to the formative use of literature is complicated by one other important ideal that characterizes the pedagogical approaches of some of the others I discussed in the previous chapter as well as my own teaching, and that formed a significant part of what motivated this study. As I've mentioned, in my classes I have long sought to involve students as knowledge producers thinking along with me about our subject and its importance, in order that they be actively involved in the learning process rather than merely observers or recipients of my learning. The question of why read literature, which would ground our exploration of that subject, was one for which I could formulate no thoughtful answer, and so I undertook this study. Now to return to that pedagogical ideal. What does it mean for a literary education that prioritizes the formative use of literature to consider students not as recipients of an education but as participants in it or contributors to it? What does it mean to attempt to accomplish these instructional objectives while at the same time placing students in the role of knowledge producers or co-inquirers?

The complication of casting students as co-inquirers
Ultimately, and simply, fully casting students as co-inquirers with their instructor means that this conception of the formative use of literature and its value is not a given in a literature course but is itself open to question as a part of the classroom community's inquiry. The questions I've asked in this study — Why read literature? What is its value? — become questions the students themselves take up. The answers at which I've arrived become one contribution to the knowledge produced through the course, albeit a substantial one, but one that confirms, develops, challenges or is challenged by the insights students themselves contribute. I've stressed the importance in literary education of expecting and enabling students to be full participants in making meaning (or making worlds) from literary texts; just as essential for a literary education to be effective is that they participate in producing the matter — the content — of the course. It is only in such involvement that learning becomes active for students and that they are invited or even required to integrate the knowledge they acquire with what they already know and do.

Other teachers of literature also discuss this shift in student roles, and some of their observations can help develop a fuller conception of its importance and of what it means for teaching. Philip Davis captures this shift in different terms. In his approach to instruction, he claims that he wants "starting points from which to work upwards, not principles from which to work down" (*Experience*, 57). Why? Principles present students with conclusions — the results of someone else's inquiry. What Davis calls "starting points" invite students to enter the inquiry from its beginning with what they know already. The knowledge or perspective students bring into the class may indeed be naïve, simplistic, or even blatantly wrong, but there is no other place from which they can start. As Davis explains, "We start from where we are at bottom, we work upwards from such foundations as we have, however rocky or risky . . . .. you are who you are, you may in that be quite lost and wrong, but you cannot be right by simply missing yourself out, as if you could transcend what you never even admitted in the first place" (*Experience*, 58). Casting students as co-inquirers in any kind of course, involving them in the activity of producing knowledge, means beginning from where they are, not where we, their instructors, are. According to Davis, this means that "we have partly to hide our own principles from ourselves and start from below them" (*Experience*, 57). A conception of the formative use of literature will therefore serve as a guide of sorts, supplying an instructor with a sense of direction for a course, but to begin by merely informing students of this capacity of literary reading is to exclude them and the knowledge they bring with them from participation in the process of inquiry. Their inclusion requires that the instructor recognize the value of whatever insights, experiences, or opinions the students have to contribute to the course, not only for the sake of the students' investment in the course and in their own learning, but also because students' insights will in fact contribute significantly to their instructor's understanding of what transpires between readers and texts. Once students are actively involved and invested in the questions which form the focus of the course's inquiry, the instructor can offer her own contributions to the investigation in which they are engaged together, taking into consideration what the students have already contributed.

When the instructor-student relationship is that of co-inquirers, the instructor's knowledge of the subject matter is, of course, still important, but the dissemination of that knowledge is no longer his primary pedagogical task. Dennis Sumara offers a formulation of what becomes the instructor's main role in this approach.

> The teacher's most important work is to create conditions whereby students are able to enter into a world of inquiry that is new and interesting. At the same time, the good teacher understands that if this world of inquiry is to remain interesting to the teacher, its

boundaries must be continually expanded to include what is not familiar to the teacher. Good teaching, then, depends upon the teacher's ability to create conditions whereby she and her students can enter into a shared world of inquiry that, while primarily organized by her, is also able to accommodate what students know and, importantly, what is generated through their shared interest.

(119)

In literary education as co-inquiry, the instructor's role is no longer primarily that of delivering the knowledge he has acquired to his students, but rather he creates conditions — both in terms of activities and environment — in which students can make discoveries and produce knowledge together with their instructor.

What are those conditions? Foremost, they include a few broad questions on which to focus together as a classroom community, questions in which students can take an interest and which encompass the primary objective of the course. For an introductory literature course one such question might be: Why does literature matter? A more advanced course might focus on a similar question but for the particular genre or period under consideration. For instance: What was the role of Renaissance drama in its time and what does it offer us today? Or: What does it take for us today to read ancient world literature and what is the good of doing so? With questions like these as a focus, the instructor must then provide students with the means for exploring them. These means consist of activities and assignments that facilitate discovery — researching outside experts' treatment of the texts or periods in question, for instance, but also the opportunity and ability to experience literary texts themselves in such a way that students can point to or hypothesize about the value or, more broadly, the effect of such experiences for them. (That students might then deny any value in their encounter with the texts in question is a possibility in this approach, and an important one for the learning of both the instructor and students, a matter I will address later in this chapter.)

Determining what conditions are necessary to enable students to take on such an inquiry requires consideration of the abilities, experiences, and interests students bring with them into the classroom. David Bleich acknowledges as much when he writes, "To take teaching seriously is to do, perhaps the opposite of 'theorizing' about it: once in class, see who is there . . . examine what people actually do, and find the curriculum, backwards, in retrospect, after the moment has been seized and class members have faced one another over time" (62). The "curriculum" that is found "backwards" is the content of the course, the accumulated knowledge and insight of students' and teacher's inquiry together. A significant part of the "curriculum" that the instructor prepares in advance, in addition to the broad objective or focus of inquiry of the course, is the means to "see who is there" and to "examine what [they] actually do", in order to begin from where the students are and to ensure that the course actually creates the conditions necessary to enable students to enter into the inquiry. One of the most significant differences between instruction as the teacher's activity and instruction as a joint inquiry between teacher and students is that in the latter formulation it matters greatly who is in the classroom with the teacher, or, more specifically, what perspectives, abilities, and experiences those particular students bring with them. What students bring into a class will necessarily affect what can and will happen in that class, and that is the next area of consideration to which I'll turn.

Making Space for Students

What students bring to the class
In order to invite and enable students to participate fully in both the inquiry of a literature course as a whole and in the encounters with literary texts which form its core, the instructor must consider the students in her classroom, as Rosenblatt had already recognized in the late 1930s. She writes,

> The teacher realistically concerned with helping his students develop a vital sense of literature cannot, then, keep his eyes focused only on the literary materials he is seeking to make available. He must also understand the personalities who are to experience this literature. He must be ready to face the fact that the students' reactions will inevitably be in terms of their own temperaments and backgrounds.
>
> (*Literature*, 50)

Students' encounters with literary texts and with the course itself will unavoidably be affected by what the students bring with them into class: their past experiences with literary texts and their assumptions about what reading them involves; their experiences of transitional objects of any kind, including currently more culturally prevalent forms like music, movies, and even video games; their experiences with life more generally, whether a class consists predominantly of eighteen- or nineteen-year-old parent-supported suburbanites, recent immigrants, older adults returning to school, or a mixture of all of these; and their past experiences with school and the expectations and habits those experiences have shaped.[7]

---

7 One unavoidable fact of some post-secondary classrooms that will challenge the instructional approach I'm advocating is class size. Considering who is in the

In a literature course, students' past experiences will influence what they will do with the course and its subject, whether or not an instructor acknowledges their effect. In regard to students' literary experience, the challenge of making meaning from a Shakespeare sonnet or one of Henry James' stories will be dramatically different for a class made up predominantly of avid readers compared to a class of students who read little or read only nonfiction. Students who have not yet discovered that literary reading can provoke an experience of any kind will need a very different kind of assistance than those who already know that literary reading can offer deeply moving experiences or that those experiences can at times come only after repeated readings of a work. Although an instructor will need to a certain extent to anticipate these areas of student need before a course begins in order to select texts and develop the basic structure of the course, an early assignment, like one Sheridan Blau uses of asking students to write brief autobiographies of themselves as readers, can give the instructor a more accurate perspective on the reading experience of those in her classroom. Inviting students to share some of their reading experiences with others in the class will foster awareness of ways in which their own experiences may be representative or exceptional and prompts a greater level of reflection on those experiences.

Students' experience with transitional objects should also be considered in a literature course concerned with texts' use in this psychic space. It seems likely that affecting encounters with literary texts cannot be taken for granted in the past reading experiences of many students, but the pervasiveness in our culture of movies, music, and video games means that most students may be familiar with (though not consciously aware of) other forms of formative experience in which they may have even acquired considerable expertise. The habits students have developed in their use of other types of transitional objects will surely influence the ways in which they expect cultural objects to function. Tapping those areas of familiarity may help students recognize, reflect on, and even move toward the kind of engaging, satisfying experience that literary reading can potentially provide, while also bringing to light assumptions that may limit their capacity to make a meaningful experience from a text. Some of the most vigorous and enthusiastic class discussions I've been part of are those occasions I've asked students to recall and talk about a book, movie, or song that grabbed them, stayed with them, or left an effect on them. Those specific memories can provide a different context from which to consider works of literature, both in recognizing the popular influence of certain texts in

classroom is obviously much easier with twenty students than with two hundred. It is, I'd like to believe, still possible and just as essential in a large lecture course to create a community of inquiry, however the methods to do so will require much creativity and experimentation, and likely a strategic use of teaching assistants.

past ages and in opening up students' expectations for ways of engaging with literature. Asking students to consider how they are affected by an especially powerful movie or a concert or a favorite video game can raise their awareness of what a literary text can make possible for an effective reader as they become more aware of the effect on them of their use of these other kinds of objects. Prompting students also to examine the frustrations they encounter in reading literature can lead them to recognize expectations they bring to a text, expectations that have been shaped by their experiences with stories in now-dominant visual forms or other more popular types of transitional objects. And then asking them to consider the differences in what the use of these various objects requires of them may help them adjust their expectations of a literary encounter. Just as significantly, their insights and observations can contribute to their instructor's education in the workings of other potentially transitional or formative cultural practices.

What students have already experienced in life generally will also significantly influence their capacity to recreate and immerse themselves in the worlds of literary texts. Any reader's life experience will to some extent determine the particular texts capable of serving as transitional objects for that reader because such use of objects depends upon a measure of resonance between the object and the individual (although those areas of resonance are ultimately impossible to predict). Many texts will not "fit" many readers, something of which teachers should often remind themselves as they select texts for students from whom they are often quite distant in life experience. Once again Rosenblatt, of course, recognized this phenomenon long ago, though without the perspective of psychoanalytic theory. She writes, "An intense response to a work will have its roots in capacities and experiences already present in the personality and mind of the reader. This principle is an important one to remember in the selection of literary materials to be presented to students. It is not enough merely to think of what the student *ought* to read" (*Literature*, 41). Rosenblatt's observation offers one possible explanation for the apparent inability of the students in a course I taught to recognize what to me seemed to be the strong though implicit criticism in Flannery O'Connor's "Everything that Rises Must Converge" of the story's protagonist, a recent college graduate who had returned home. In a class discussion I asked students in a number of different ways about their own sense of that character and their sense of the text's view of the character, and, though there was much discussion, no one pointed out the text's critique of the character that I found so obvious. It occurred to me later that perhaps these students, all very early in their college careers, may have been too close themselves to the life situation of that character to perceive what I saw as the text's stance toward him (that portion of the text's "protocol"). While it may have been possible for these students to come to some awareness of the tone of O'Connor's story, it would have required more careful assistance than I had anticipated or was able in the moment to offer. In selecting texts and planning what we ask of students regarding them, it's important not only that we consider students' reading abilities, but that we also remain mindful of the life experience necessary for students to recreate the world of a text.

Even more than their life experience, students' interactions with literary texts and the roles they are willing to take in the literature classroom itself will be shaped by their schooling, what they perceive they have been expected — implicitly or explicitly — to do in school. In fact I've found this factor to be the greatest challenge in my own efforts to experiment with an alternative instructional model. Sheridan Blau captures the effect he has seen on students in his classes of their previous literature instruction.

> When they are asked to talk about a text in class . . . they act like witnesses to a crime who are afraid of being personally involved or have been warned by a judge to stick to the facts and not draw any inferences or reach any conclusions of their own. They generally suspect that they are supposed to do more than provide a mere plot summary, but they seem not to know what else there is to say in an academic context that isn't either plot summary or else the predictable pseudoacademic observations encouraged by study guides and, unfortunately, by some typical school assignments.
>
> (102)

What Blau's students carried away from their earlier schooling had convinced them that their own responses to the texts they read did not belong in the classroom, leaving them at a loss to know what to say about a text in school. An open assignment, like writing a response of their own to their reading of a text, will frustrate students for whom school work is largely a matter of figuring out "what the teacher wants". In my own teaching experience, the assumption I've found most difficult for some students to relinquish is the view that learning takes place only when one who knows tells that knowledge to those who don't know (a view that matches the teacherly version I discussed early in the previous chapter).

While not all students will have internalized the same assumptions about what is expected of them in a literature classroom, all of them will enter our classrooms with some preconceived and largely tacit notions of their role, both regarding what reading and discussing literature or any texts in school involves, and what behaviors are expected of them in a classroom. If an instructor wants students to take up a role different from that of their past schooling experiences, he must be mindful of the expectations students bring with them and intentionally seek ways to intervene, to redirect those expectations. They may need the differences between the new expectations and the old explicitly addressed, to be prompted to talk about their past literature instruction in order to make its assumptions explicit and to reflect on them. Students may be otherwise resistant, for instance, to bring into the classroom through their discussion and their writing their own confusion or frustration with texts, or powerful and personal connections they may have experienced in reading that they may expect to be unimportant in an academic context or too risky to admit. In an educational approach informed by the formative use of literature, these individual aspects of a reading experience are not the sole interest of a course, but they do play an essential role and so need to be welcomed.

In addition to making visible for students through explicit discussion the ways in which a course requires a shift in expectations, an instructor needs also to design classroom activities that will facilitate that shift by intentionally placing students in new roles. Marshall, Smagorinsky, and Smith's study of high school English classrooms documented the difficulty of carrying out in practice one's pedagogical ideals, as they observed the tendency of teacher and students alike to fall back on a more traditional "speech genre" in class interaction. They conclude, "The influence of the speech genre of classroom discussions of literature suggests that we are most likely to change the way the people talk about literature in school not simply by changing the instructional moves we make during discussion, but rather by devising activities and situations that demand that teachers and students take on new roles" (132). They add, "What we are suggesting is not so much that teachers resist the speech genre we have described in our studies, though we applaud such efforts, but rather that they subvert it by creating contexts in which it does not apply" (134). It may not be sufficient to expect students to take on new roles in a literature classroom merely because we ask them to. If we want students to immerse themselves in the textual worlds they recreate and to contribute to the class's inquiry whatever they learn from those textual encounters, we need to create assignments and classroom situations in which students are not able to maintain the more passive role of receiving and repeating the knowledge of experts, and which also prompt them to recognize the gains in knowledge that can come through comparing and reflecting on the experience of peers. A writing assignment Blau uses asks students to report on whatever they notice themselves doing as they read an unfamiliar short text. Because their own reading process is the focus of the assignment, students themselves become the sources of their own research. Sharing these assignments with others in the class shifts the focus of classroom attention from the finished products of the instructor's or critics' literary analysis to the work-in-progress of students' readings, and requires students to focus on and talk about their own experience of making something of a text. When an instructor does not attempt to counteract the expectations of schooling that students bring into the classroom through assignments she creates, she leaves her intentions for the course vulnerable to a significant source of potential resistance that can easily undermine what she hopes to accomplish. Addressing these expectations explicitly through classroom discussion and experientially by creating tasks and situations that require new roles can diffuse much of that resistance and encourage students to take the risks new roles involve.

In this fairly extensive discussion of the expectations and experiences that students bring into a literature course, it is important to remember that the instructor herself is also a member of this community of inquiry with countless assumptions, expectations, and experiences of her own. As she considers the experiences with reading, with transitional objects, with life in general, and with schooling that her students bring into the classroom, it is just as necessary for her to consider her own experience in all of these realms so that she can be as aware as possible of all that she carries into the classroom and that will inevitably contribute to what can and will happen in the course.

However, it is not only what students and teacher bring to a literature course at its outset that matters when literature instruction seeks to foster formative experience. At least of equal significance is that the classroom remains a safe and welcoming setting for students to risk making on-going contributions, one additional area of consideration.

A receptive environment for students' contributions

If a literature course is to be a joint inquiry between students and teacher in which students' potentially formative experiences with the texts of the course are to be a central focus, it is essential that the classroom remain an environment receptive to whatever students have to contribute, especially their perspective on their experiences with texts. Establishing and maintaining that environment is the instructor's responsibility, within the context of his accountability both to the subject of study and to the institution of which the course is a part, and this means that the instructor remains the ultimate decision-maker in the classroom. The openness of the classroom to student contributions does not mean that the instructor abdicates his authority, a requirement of the learning environment that is important for students to understand while they are in the process of reorienting their expectations for their role in the classroom. Though an instructor's decisions within a course must satisfy the needs of the institution and accommodate the subject of study as he understands it, the area of consideration that is more easily overlooked is that which will facilitate the continued openness of the classroom environment to students' involvement.

The central contribution students can make to a literature course is an account of their own encounters with literary texts. Recognition of the importance to a literary education of students' experiences with texts brings opportunity for students to move out of the passive role of recipients of others' knowledge. Instead, as Sheridan Blau observes, "The students become valued experts because only they can know and can report on their own experiences as readers engaged with the problems they encounter" (13). A first consideration then in maintaining a classroom environment receptive to this expertise of students, as well as a key to fostering students' potential formative use of texts, is that students be initially allowed to have *their own* experiences of texts, which they are invited to bring into the classroom. In addressing the instructional objectives of this approach to literary education, I've already discussed the importance of students reading the texts themselves. Here I'd like to examine how that priority affects a teacher's role.

The way an instructor introduces a text or prepares students to read it can unintentionally limit or precondition students' encounters with that text, thus restricting the text's availability as a transitional object for them and possibly preventing them from constructing a world from the text themselves at all by constraining beforehand what they are able to make of the text. James Seitz points out the effect of the nature of an assignment on students' written work when he writes, "As readers of student writing, we occupy the peculiar position of having sharply curtailed, through our 'assignments', the possibilities for the texts we read before they even come to be written" (329). Similarly, with students' reading, what we ask of them beforehand or how we prepare them for the reading assignment will shape their expectations of the text and therefore what they are able to do or see in their reading. The narrowness of our expectations, shaped by our own reading experiences, will mold theirs and so determine the possibilities of that text for them. Should we be able to free students as much as possible from our own unavoidably limited expectations of a text, what they produce may in fact broaden our own perspectives (though, of course, students' "free" readings are free only in the present moment, having already been determined by their various past experiences with literature and with school).

This is not to say, however, that students will not need at times significant assistance in making something of a text nor that the readings they produce will necessarily be without obvious misreadings. Yet another return to Rosenblatt offers some important clarifications between providing students assistance in reading and preventing them from having a reading of their own. She writes,

> [A primary duty is] not to impose a set of preconceived notions about the proper way to react to any work. The student must be free to grapple with his own reaction. This primary negative condition does not mean that the teacher abdicates his duty to attempt to

instill sound habits of reading or sound critical attitudes. Nor does this imply that historical and biographical background material will be neglected. The difference is that instead of trying to superimpose routine patterns, the teacher will help students develop these understandings in the context of their own emotions and their own curiosity about life and literature.

(*Literature*, 63)

Visible in Rosenblatt's admonition for literature instructors is the relationship between immersive and reflective reading I put forward in Chapter 2, that reading moves which involve stepping back from the text for some form of reflection on it gain meaning or significance only in the context of the reader's immersive reading, her experience of the text's world as she recreates it (or struggles to do so).[8] Knowledge that the instructor can and should provide, such as background information about a text, will, in Rosenblatt's words, "have value only when the student feels the need of it and when it is assimilated into the student's experience of particular literary works" (*Literature*, 117). What will provoke in students a felt need for what the instructor has to offer? Their own experience of attempting to make meaning from a text.

The instructor's responsibility is, then, first to provide students the opportunity to make what they can of a text and to reflect on that experience (the experience of both the text's world and the process of recreating it). The "reading" a student produces and her response to it can then become key sources of learning when she is invited to share them with others in the class, and together students encounter varied ways of making meaning from texts and varied results of those efforts. As I've claimed, exposure to others' perspectives on a text provoke fuller awareness of what literary reading involves and what it makes possible. Creating this opportunity is the instructor's second task, as Rosenblatt explains.

Having created the environment for evoking an experienced meaning and reacting freely to it, the teacher then seeks to create a situation in which the student becomes aware of possible alternative interpretations and responses and is led to examine further both his own reaction and the text itself. In this way he is helped to understand his own preoccupations and assumptions better. He considers whether he has overlooked elements in the text. He thus becomes more aware of the various verbal clues — the diction, the

---

8   Rosenblatt's terms for contrasting reading modes, aesthetic and efferent, correlate with my use of immersive and reflective reading, but they emphasize the focus of a reader's attention rather than his psychological location in relation to the text.

rhythmic pattern, structure, and symbol — and develops or deepens his understanding of concepts such as voice, persona, point of view, genre.

(*Literature*, 214)

A discussion of differences in what one another has made of a text can produce in students a fuller awareness of features of the text, as Rosenblatt observes. But, as I've claimed, in a classroom of diverse students a discussion of differences in readings can also provoke an increased recognition of the influence of different readers' cultural locations on their experiences of the text. Through student reflection and interaction, the critical content of a literature course can emerge, but not as knowledge which students passively receive from their instructor and must assimilate on their own. Rather, students produce the knowledge themselves through what they notice in one another's readings with the facilitation of their instructor, and they experience its value as means of enriching their own encounters with the literary texts under discussion.

To maximize the potential of literary works to serve as transitional objects, students' felt experiences of the textual worlds they produce must be solicited in class assignments and discussion as much as the more scholarly type of considerations they may have become accustomed to in other schooling contexts. Hearing what others have experienced can both deepen students' own sense of a text's world and also help them to develop an understanding more generally of the transaction between text and reader.

If the classroom is to be receptive to students' experiences of texts and reflections on those experiences, and to whatever else they have to contribute, the instructor must become adept at accommodating and respecting the unexpected. This is a second consideration in maintaining a classroom environment of receptivity, after ensuring that students are allowed to have their own experiences of texts and to bring accounts of them into class discussion. In my own experience as an instructor it did not take long for me to discover that asking for students' input could quickly result in contributions that left me at times dumbfounded, so far were they from what I expected students to say. I also learned that my response to such offerings would in large part determine students' willingness to continue to risk speaking up as well as my own opportunity to learn from my students both about the process of teaching and about our subject itself. If difference can breed awareness and thus learning, we ought not to expect only our students to undergo such growth. The primary opportunity for the instructor's learning in the classroom is when she is faced with responses from students that counter her expectations, contributions that require her to think again about her subject or her teaching. Keeping the classroom, and more particularly the instructor's own attitude, receptive and responsive to such surprises is central to a literary education that casts students as co-inquirers and one that prioritizes the unique, individual interaction with a text that makes possible the formative use of literary reading.

What does such receptivity involve? It requires a reorientation of what is valued in the classroom. What will initially prove to be the greatest contribution to the classroom community's learning is reports (or admissions) of what actually happened as class members encountered the printed page. In Rosenblatt's words, "Frank expression of boredom or even vigorous rejection is a more valid starting point for learning than are docile attempts to feel 'what the teacher wants'" (*Literature*, 67). Because a student in a freshman-level class I was teaching was bold enough to tell his small group, in my hearing, that he found a Flannery O'Connor story to be "a waste of time" when he had midterms to study for, I had the chance to learn that my starting point with that student and likely some others was much different than I had expected. He could make so little sense of the beginning of the story that he saw no reason to continue working through it. His remark also produced the opportunity for another student in his group to describe the effect she experienced of leaving the story for a time and coming back to it later, leading the group of students to a discussion of strategies for approaching texts they found difficult. In the instructional approach I'm advocating, "wrong" answers and outright resistance become essential opportunities for identifying obstacles students face in making something of a text and for beginning to work through them, while they also reveal more about the interaction between text and reader.

At the same time, what may seem to be resistance or disinterest from students may mean something entirely different, as Slatoff points out. He writes, ". . . while silence, inarticulateness, and confusion on the part of our students may indicate a lack of sufficient response and understanding, they may not mean that at all and may sometimes be signs that the experience has been particularly meaningful, complex, or full" (177). He goes on to remind us as teachers that the very qualities we tend to value, "the stated, the rational, the articulate, the orderly, the explicit, and the precise" often involve, in his words, "a reduction of experience and reality and a certain sacrifice of richness, complexity, and truth" (178). Confusion, inarticulateness, or silence in students may indeed mean something quite different from the insufficient interaction with the text that we might expect it to mean. Allowing for alternative interpretations of students' classroom contributions (or lack of contribution) requires that instructors listen well, which means in part learning to hesitate in drawing conclusions and to tolerate some uncertainty that can feel uncomfortable when a classroom full of students' eyes are on one, looking for what to do next. Our own insecurity with seemingly awkward classroom moments and our need to maintain control of class interaction can prevent us from recognizing and making room for what may potentially be some of the most valuable or meaningful contributions students have to offer.

Yet instructors are not the only ones who need to learn to respect and listen to what may initially seem insufficient. Students themselves need prompting to reconsider the validity of their own responses, an endeavor Philip Davis considers a key part of a teacher's responsibility. He writes,

> The first task of the teacher in the class was to ensure that the men and women there knew that, somewhere in themselves, they did 'have a reason' for their strongest reactions, that they were implicitly thinking; the second task was to lead them towards writing which sought to find and give the reason which they somewhere had. In real writing and thinking, what is implicit or pre-articulate comes first; the explicit is the struggle in the second place to bring to light, under the pen, all that is anterior to itself.
>
> ("Place", 154)

Davis's conception of the teacher's task implies that even the student in my class who concluded that the Flannery O'Connor story was a waste of time was indeed implicitly thinking — that he had a reason for his reaction, stemming from his expectations for the development of a story that did not fit what he found in O'Connor's work, and it was a reason that was important for our (his and my) learning. Though a course should certainly help students move beyond responses like that of this student, it can best do so when teacher and students alike attend to the thinking implicit in such responses. Students' past schooling experiences will not likely have fostered such attention, and so students may require considerable prompting to reflect on their responses.[9]

As Davis suggests, writing is well suited for such reflection because of the time and attention it involves. But the writing capable of fostering this kind of reflection will not likely be polished at least in its initial form. Students' struggle to express the inarticulate will be impeded if they believe they must at the same time produce only well-crafted thesis-driven essays. Blau, in *The Literature Workshop*, advocates using other kinds of writing in literature courses as well as the traditional essay, including reading logs and reports on students' own reading process, that may better serve this function. The more informal reading

---

9   A related challenge that I haven't yet found a way to resolve is in helping students recognize and value the thinking implicit in one another's responses, a task made more difficult (or perhaps impossible) by the unfortunate tendency of some students to invest very little effort in reading for the course, especially compared to the work of others.

log allows students to keep a record of their experiences with texts while the reading process report, which I mentioned earlier, pushes them to examine and describe what it is they do as they work to make something of an unfamiliar text. (Later in this chapter I will describe my own use of informal writing assignments like these.) Accommodating, respecting, and attending to the unexpected from students in a literature classroom, and helping students to do the same themselves is a necessary means of ensuring that students' own experiences with texts have a place in the classroom, and it maximizes opportunities for learning for students and teacher alike.

However, involving students in the production of knowledge in a literature course does not mean that course content is limited to only what students themselves happen to notice and contribute. An instructor still has means to ensure that matters she deems necessary get included in what transpires in the classroom. One way is by crafting tasks that prompt students to notice what the instructor wants introduced in class discussion. Having students read two or three texts that differ markedly in the distance at which they place their audience, for instance, will bring attention to that technique and its effect. In her Renaissance drama course, as I mentioned in the previous chapter, Francis Teague has found that she can prompt students to realize how the plays on which her course focuses don't fit their expectations for plot by intentionally giving them an assignment that asks them to identify in the plays elements of plot that they in fact lack. Her students' learning thus comes through the impossibility of the assignment they attempt. (One of the few specific lessons I've never forgotten from my first year of college came through just that sort of impossible assignment. It stayed with me more vividly than any other assignment I was given that year.) These are just a few examples of ways an instructor can design tasks or activities that enable students to discover what she wants to teach them rather than just hearing about it from her.

That is not to say, however, that there is no room in this instructional approach for teaching in the form of telling students something — including the lecture. Another way that an instructor can introduce into class discussion what she thinks needs to be included is by offering it herself, but with two conditions different from the more traditional teacher-student relationship. If the course is constructed to be a joint inquiry, then students need to be included as co-inquirers before the instructor supplies her own answers to the questions about which the course is concerned. Once students have themselves begun to investigate the questions at hand, it is likely they will eagerly welcome whatever the instructor has to contribute to the inquiry in which they are already engaged. Within the context of their inquiry, the instructor becomes one more resource for potential answers to *their* questions.

That the instructor is *one more* resource for answers points to a second difference from the more traditional model of instruction. Rather than serving as the only authority in the classroom, here the instructor is one authority among many, both among the students themselves — whose degree of authority derives from their own experiences with texts — and among other experts outside the classroom to whom students may gain access through their investigation. The instructor need not only attempt to elicit from students whatever insights he wants to see included in the course, but, as a co-inquirer himself within the course, he can offer his perspective as well, remaining mindful of the extra weight it will (and should) carry because of his position. To maintain an environment of joint inquiry, the instructor should make his own contributions to the knowledge produced in the course strategically, filling in gaps that can't otherwise be covered easily, and careful to guard the authority of students' own experiences and their ability to question their instructor. The instructor's contributions can also assist in setting the tone for a class discussion by modeling the type of comments she would like to have students offer. I will sometimes begin a discussion, for instance, by expressing my own shock at some particularly outrageous portion of a text, implicitly inviting students to offer reactions of their own before turning the focus to a more typical analysis of the role such a passage might play in the text overall. In a course in which students are cast as knowledge producers and their experiences reading literary texts are to play an essential part, the instructor can and should still maintain significant influence over the content (the knowledge) that emerges from the course by the tasks she designs for students to perform and by her own contributions as a participant in the inquiry.

Asking students to involve themselves actively in this way in both classroom interaction and in the reading of literature necessarily carries with it some risk for them. A final consideration in maintaining a classroom environment of receptivity is that the literature classroom be a safe place for students to take these risks. This requires that the instructor stay alert to the very real potential for emotional harm when students make themselves vulnerable by speaking openly in class and by subjecting themselves to the literary texts they read. Awareness of this possibility comes from a shift in perspective that Deanne Bogdan articulates as a reconceptualization of the goal of literary education from "something that has to do with reading and studying literature in the abstract to that which is accountable for the concrete consequences of students as embodied learners" (159). If we as instructors invite students' involvement in the literature classroom, it will become difficult — and counterproductive — to ignore the presence of the very real and very diverse human beings in the room who will affect and be affected by what transpires. Because the instructor is in the position of greatest power in the classroom, able to a significant extent to choose what she will ask of students, it is her responsibility to be mindful of the possible effects on students of her requests and to prevent potential harm as best she can.

One possible source of harm when students are asked to speak openly of their reading experiences and reflections on them is the nature of the interaction that will surround their contributions. If an instructor asks students to risk offering their own perspectives and encourages class discussion of those contributions, it is imperative that he both models and demands respect in classroom interaction. If students' input — whatever it may be — is not safe from ridicule or reproach, they will wisely avoid speaking up. The teacher, as the host of the classroom, sets and maintains the tone and can remedy affronts by his response to any unkind or insensitive remarks others might make. Past experiences of shame or humiliation in school can produce in students on-going anxiety that will undermine their willingness to take such risks again. I was fortunate early in my teaching experience to have a student write in a class assignment of the fear that overtook her every time she put her hand on the door knob of our classroom, knowing that once inside she would be expected to talk. Though I believe it was still important for me to push this very quiet international student to speak up in class, it was invaluable for me to hear that she found the experience terrifying because it enabled me to be more mindful of what she was undergoing and broadened my capacity to imagine the experiences of others in my classes.

But classroom interaction is no greater risk than subjecting oneself to a text when a literary education actively seeks to make possible formative experiences with literature. Bogdan's attention to embodied readers "affected by the specificities of our feeling, power, and location" — or in other words our varied and varying emotional states, positions of power, and the cultural sites we occupy — prompts her to recognize the risk we undergo when we allow boundaries to loosen in literary reading (192). As I discussed in Chapter 2, Bogdan understands that the unique potential of literary reading for destabilizing students' senses of themselves gives teachers of literature "an awesome responsibility" in creating a pedagogical context which provides "a safe psychic and social environment" (192). A part of creating that safe environment for student readers is recognizing that the transformational capacity of literary reading will have the potential to provoke discomfort in students if they are able to undertake the kinds of encounters with texts we hope for them, and, more importantly, that that discomfort may be more than some students are ready or able to bear. Of course, learning is rarely a comfortable process and making it such should not be a goal, but we as instructors can too easily disregard or underestimate the trauma students potentially suffer whose lives are removed from our own.

The student who saw a positive ending in a story where I and others in the class felt a pervasive sense of loss was able to account for the reading he produced by pointing to the similarity between Jhumpa Lahiri's story, "Mrs. Sen's", and his own life experience. Like the young boy at the end of Lahiri's text, my student stayed home alone after school as a pre-adolescent when his single mother had decided he was old enough to no longer need a sitter. For this student, the loss the text conveys of the boy's relationship with his caregiver, Mrs. Sen, was entirely overshadowed by the compliment to his growing maturity implied in his mother's decision to leave him home alone. This story was about a mother's confidence in her son, my student insisted, because, as he explained, that is how he understood his own experience of being left home alone after school. In writing about this classroom discussion, a significant number of students wrote that they realized how different people can read the same story very differently. As the instructor, I, on the other hand, realized how threatening a story can be when it potentially calls into question one's interpretation of one's own life experience. This student's resistance to attending to the details in the text that pointed to a different interpretation may have been his defense against the possibility of having his own conception of himself undermined. As his instructor, pushing him toward that possibility could carry consequences of greater ethical import than his learning to read a literary text. Teaching literature with care for students' vulnerability would mean, in situations like this, pointing out that one can set aside one's own perspective momentarily in order to investigate the perspective of a text — allowing the possibility that my student's similar experience can be affirming while the text's event at the same time can be one of loss. However, even this move may have been too threatening for this particu-lar student, and a position like his needs to be given space if the classroom is going to remain receptive and safe for students' contributions and for students themselves. If literary reading is indeed capable of producing the formative effects I've described in earlier chapters, then the potential psychological impact of inviting students into such encounters with texts cannot be ignored. Treading into such territory demands delicacy, out of respect for the very real human beings who venture with us.

If a literary education is going to be conducive to students' formative encounters with literature, then one of its primary objectives is to make space for those students to experience as fully as they can the worlds of the texts they read, for only in that experience can a literary work become a transitional object. What students need in order to create their own experience of a literary work depends on who those students are and what they bring with them into the classroom. Their varied experiences with the works they read take a central place in a course as the differences (and similarities) between those experiences become a central source of their learning about the texts and the way they work, about cultures, and about themselves. Instruction can no longer be conceived of mainly as the instructor's activity, nor can a course remain preoccupied with the critical or scholarly to the neglect of readers' experiences of a text's world. Literature instruction can make literary texts available for students' use as objects in transitional space when it prioritizes immersive reading as it is supported and enhanced by reflective reading, when it involves students as co-inquirers and experts in their own textual encounters, when it is mindful of the experiences students bring into the classroom with texts and other transitional objects, with schooling, and with life itself, and finally when it provides a receptive and safe environment for students' on-going, often unexpected contributions. So what might a literature class based on these ideals look like in practice? In what follows I'll explain briefly how I currently work to enact these principles in the courses I teach.

Ideas for Practice

As joint inquiries with students, my courses center around a couple of broad questions, as I mentioned earlier, questions to which students will formulate their own answers by the semester's end. "What does reading literature involve and why does it matter?" in an introductory course or, in a course on classics of Western literature in translation, "Why do you think these works have been so influential and why should they continue to be read — or why not?" (I always include in some form a question about literature's value, not only because it's of greatest interest to me, but also because students can begin to identify its value when they first wonder about it.) With inquiry questions like these as the focus, the core of my classes is a multi-part reading journal that students keep, certainly not a novel idea in itself, but one that serves several different functions in the approach to literature instruction that I've described above. In this journal, kept on loose-leaf paper so that I can collect and read portions of it, students gather their initial reactions to the literary works we read, their notes on class discussions and presentations, and reflections they write that pull together all we've done with each particular text. Then ultimately the journals serve as sourcebooks from which they draw their own claims in answer to the course's inquiry questions.

The first type of journal entry consists of informal reactions to each reading assignment given in the class. Students describe what their reading experience was like — their experience both of the process of reading the text and of the imaginary world they create or attempt to create through their reading. These entries become the means by which students' initial experiences reading an assigned work become part of the course as the ground on which we build together. They bring what they've written into class to share with a small group for comparison with others' experiences of the text and to discuss together any challenges they faced in the reading. I also collect these entries and read through them myself, using the questions or observations students mention to direct the activities of the following class sessions that will focus on the particular literary work. The assignment also prevents students from merely reading passively, proceeding through the words on the page without much engagement. Martin Bickman, another who has students write informal responses to their reading, describes this benefit: "Writing about what one has read moves the whole process into a fuller dimension and makes the act of reading more active, deliberate, intense, and closely related to one's immediate experience" (155–56). A number of students have confirmed this effect in saying that they think more or pay attention more as they're reading when they know that have to write something afterward. Many have also said that they appreciate writing the reaction in place of quiz over a reading assignment because they read differently when they expect a quiz — imagining the questions as they read and searching for the answers (a sure way to hinder potential immersion in a text).

While the process of writing a reaction entry will hopefully pull students into a deeper engagement with the literary work, I deliberately leave the instructions for the assignment as open as possible. I want to allow students to attend to whatever struck them about the text and their experience of it, rather than directing their writing toward certain aspects of it and so determining ahead of time where their attention will fall. The openness of this assignment serves two purposes. First, it allows differences in students' approaches to a work to emerge so that, when they compare one another's reactions, it can provoke increased awareness of others' varied ways of reading and what those alternatives can produce. Exposure to those reading differences also fosters greater self-awareness of the assumptions they each bring to an encounter with a literary work. Second, and more significant for the formative use of literature, is that such openness makes space for students to experience and acknowledge any of the unexpected and even uncanny areas of resonance that may occur and that are essential facilitators of transitional experience. One of my students was moved beyond words by the *Aeneid*'s depiction of Dido's destructive grief. Not only is an experience like that important for a reader, but it can become a valuable piece of evidence in a class's understanding of the potential effects of literary reading, should a student be willing to share it. It needs to be both welcomed and protected in a classroom that also includes those for whom Dido's suicide is only a selfish tantrum and those who can't sufficiently get past the tedious detail of the *Aeneid* in order to engage with the text at all.

That said, the reaction assignment is one I often re-evaluate as its openness is a frustration for some students who want more direction in both their writing and their reading from an assignment like this. In Bickman's use of response journals, he asks students to answer carefully constructed, open-ended questions designed to guide them in making sense of a particular text. Referring to himself and the team of graduate students with whom he taught an undergraduate literature course, Bickman describes how they structured the journal questions.

> . . . we as teachers tried to focus on the processes by which we as readers came to an understanding of the text — for example, what words and images are repeated, what more becomes revealed in the first paragraph after one has read through the entire text, what effects are created by the syntax and rhythms of sentences — rather than on final interpretations. We asked one another what came to be known as the epistemological question: not what we know, but how we came to know it"

(156).

Based on their own processes of interpretation, the specific questions Bickman and his team craft for their students teach them how to read the literary work by directing their attention strategically. The approach seems like an effective one and one that many students would welcome. Because the questions are intentionally open-ended, students actively take part in constructing meaning from the text and thereby also constructing their own learning. Yet Bickman's assignment differs from mine in its purpose. My version deals with a more preliminary stage of reading and seeks to make space for the experience of the unexpected, letting students choose what they notice. Guidance in making sense of the literary work will follow in class, in response to whatever students have chosen to write in their reaction entries.

I place a priority on allowing students, whenever possible, to choose — whether it's what aspect of their reading experience they dwell on in their informal writing, which of a course's texts they use as a focus for a research project, or which selection from an anthology they read for an open assignment toward the end of the semester. Student choice matters in literature instruction not only because students do better work when it's of interest to them, but also because of the role of choice in the use of transitional objects. When we have been given opportunity, we are capable of choosing objects (or practices) whose shape or feel is fitted to our own usually unconscious needs. This has helped me understand why I chose as the focus of my Master's thesis T. S. Eliot's *Four Quartets*, a work that had done little more than mystify me when I encountered it twice before in my education. I didn't know why, but I felt that I somehow needed that poem and wanted to understand it. Through working on the poem for my thesis, portions of it took on such significance for me that they still come to mind often a couple of decades later. It is this kind of use of literature that motivates me to invite students to choose whenever possible, including the very open reaction entry I assign as a beginning step, a way to see into a text on students own terms. Yet some students do struggle with the lack of direction, and so I at times consider providing questions to guide their writing. What repeatedly brings me back to the open reaction assignment is the thought that something striking or peculiar or in any way interesting might occur between a student and a text, and I would hate to miss hearing about it or to miss an opportunity to let the student attempt to put it into words by limiting the focus of her writing. Even more, I would hate to limit the focus of her attention by directing it elsewhere through the assignment and so prevent what might be possible in her reading experience.

Nevertheless, most of my students still need guidance and support in their reading of most of the texts I assign, and that important step begins when students interact with each other in small groups about the reactions they've written. It then becomes the full focus of class sessions after I've read those journal entries. Whatever confusions or obstacles seem to stand out in students' writings determines subsequent class discussions. After reading that numerous students were perplexed to find that the *Iliad* doesn't include the story of the Trojan horse or Achilles' death or the fall of Troy, we examined what Homer's work did include. The class listed the major events of the epic, adding those that occur before the scene of the beginning and after the scene of the end. Then we discussed what the arc of the plot, especially the choice of where to start the story and where to end it, might suggest about its subject. Also worth exploring is what our discomfort at a story that doesn't end where we expect suggests about us. In another course, students expressed bewilderment at certain odd repeated details in Morrison's *Song of Solomon* — striking uses of the color red, for instance, or the unusual ways of naming people as I mentioned earlier. In the next class session we listed as many of these details on the board as students noticed and then chose one to follow, looking for every reference we could find and reading its context in order to speculate about its significance. Students eventually take up analyses like these on their own through an assignment that asks them to examine some puzzling or interesting feature of one of the texts we've read, without relying on outside sources, and to see what it enables them to see in the text, writing up their findings in an essay.

But reading literary works is also helped by outside information, and so students each do a research project related to one of the course's texts (of their choice again) that brings together knowledge or insight from other sources which will supplement our reading, usually answering questions that have come up in their reading. They pull together their research in the form of a paper and, perhaps more importantly, a presentation to the class so that everyone can benefit from what they've learned. The subject of the course shapes the direction of students' research. In the ancient world literature class, students investigate the cultures from which the texts come or whatever can be learned about the origins of specific texts. Someone usually focuses on gender roles in ancient Greece and informs the class that in that culture a husband's extramarital sexual activity was expected and not considered an act of unfaithfulness. In a course on key texts in translation in Western literature, students research either a text's origin or its influence — anything that's been done with it since it was written. A memorable presentation in that course offered a cogent answer to the class's question of why Dante's *Inferno* gets so much more attention than the other two parts of the *Divine Comedy*. Another explored whether Ovid's *Metamorphoses* is really considered to be humorous, since none in our class found it so. In an introductory literature course, students use scholars' work to answer a question they have about a text (like how the violence of Flannery O'Connor's stories fits with her Christian faith) or they look at what scholars have done with a text to see what they find that's interesting or helpful.[10] The reading journal plays a part in all of this work as well. The second type of entry, following a student's reaction to the text, consists of the daily notes students take on their small group interactions, whole class discussions, other students' presentations, and on the insights they gain from their own analysis and research. Together these components of a course form the second movement in Ricoeur's paradigm: standing at a distance from a text to better understand it.

In an ideal world, after all this analysis and research, we would read the *Odyssey* or Morrison's *Song of Solomon* all over again for a fuller experience of immersion in its world, Ricoeur's "second naiveté". Unfortunately that's unrealistic for all but the most unusual of students, so I instead ask them to reread their initial reactions and the notes they've kept on a specific text, looking back through the text itself as well, and then to write a reflection about that process and what they've gained, the third type of journal entry and one that's almost as open as the first. I'll read through these reflections, not to grade them, but to keep myself informed of how the class is doing with the literary works of the course.[11] Once the reflection is written for the last text the class will consider, the reading journals

---

10   In a recent article in *Pedagogy*, as I mentioned in Chapter 4, Kathleen McCormick describes her use of students' research projects to support the class's reading in her course on *Ulysses*. It is, admittedly, more thoroughly developed than my own version, and I highly recommend the article for those interested in exploring this kind of project.

11   Grading journal entries is a sure way to turn them into writing only to meet the teacher's expectations. I usually make assignments like these credit/no credit, and give credit if they are done with at least some evidence both of thought and of having read the text itself, though the latter is impossible to determine with any certainty.

are ready to serve as a sort of sourcebook that students use to help them answer the inquiry questions on which the course is focused (and this means the nature of these questions requires careful thought to ensure that students can arrive at some conclusions, however speculative). Their answers to these questions in essay form take the place of a final exam in my classes. As evidence and illustration of their claims, students draw not only on the class's analysis and research, but also on their own reading experiences. Through this means I hope students will see literature not as some solely academic subject disconnected from themselves, but as an ancient and current human practice that can change them as it changes their conceptions of themselves and of the world around them.

Yet this final essay keeps students still standing at a distance from the literary texts themselves as they reflect on them, not the position from which literature gains its power and appeal. At the end of a course, students also need opportunity and even provocation to move past thinking about literature and toward immersing themselves in it again, this time informed by all the work the class has undertaken. I have been experimenting with ways to push students toward this type of appropriation of a literary work, inhabiting it or making it a part of oneself. One way I've attempted this is by encouraging students to make a portion of a text literally "their own" through choosing a passage from one of the texts we've read to memorize. Though memorization and recitation have largely fallen out of favor in academic literary study, one powerful way to blur the boundary between self and text is to learn "by heart" a piece of that text and to speak it. According to poet Billy Collins, "To memorize is not only to possess something, whether it be a poem or a succession of kings. It is to make what is memorized an almost physical part of us, to turn it into a companion." The words that we choose to become a part of us also give us a unique form of contact with another being as we embody the words of others by giving them voice. To repeat Charles Altieri's claims about speaking the words of a poem, which I mentioned in Chapter 1: ". . . there is no better access to other identities, or to who we become because we can take on other identities, than giving ourselves over to a range of speaking voices. Then we are not watching characters on a screen or a stage; we are actually becoming the voices through which they live" (83). Through "voicing" others' words, Altieri adds, "We feel intensely what it means to enact the situations of others within our own beings" (90). Memorizing and reciting lines from a literary work allow a reader both to possess and to inhabit those words and the voice to which they give form, offering the sort of merging with the "other" of the text that is at the heart of formative reading.

As appealing as this description of the practice may sound, most students will not likely welcome the opportunity to memorize and recite anything. If those in my classes are at all typical, many have had negative experiences with memorization in their past schooling. The primary ways I attempt to counteract those bad memories involve, again, choice. Students choose which lines from which text they would like to memorize according to what most resonates for them, increasing the likelihood that the passage and the experience will feel personally meaningful. (Incidentally, discovering which passages they choose becomes an intriguing learning opportunity for their instructor.) To avoid over-burdening those for whom memorization is unfamiliar or drudgery, students also choose the length of the selection with a relatively short minimum requirement (eight or ten lines perhaps) and extra credit opportunities for those who take on something longer. I also suggest that students write out the lines they plan to learn on a small piece of paper that they can carry with them or post in a prominent place to read over repeatedly, preferably over a couple of weeks. Not only does frequent re-reading produce a familiarity that eases the process of memorization, it also allows students to become immersed not just in the story world of a text but also in the specific words themselves and the feeling state embodied in their sounds and rhythm. Then for those terrified of reciting in front of the class, I make that an optional exercise. What counts for their grade is what they are able to write out from memory. They then give "voice" to the words they've learned before two or three other students, a much less intimidating situation, and we all encourage everyone willing to recite or perform their passage for the class to do so. This serves as a fitting end-of-semester activity because it bestows value on passages from the texts read during a course as we hear them from one another, specific words in a specific order worth holding on to.

A second way I've tried to prompt students to appropriate the texts of a literature course, and another way to celebrate them, is by asking students to recreate or re-envision something they've read for our class. Having students produce a piece of creative writing inspired by a literary work may not be an unusual assignment, but I've opened it to other media in hopes of more fully engaging students whose imaginative strengths and inclinations may lie outside the written word. What emerges, especially from students skilled in some form of artistic expression, is what might be considered an internalized text made tangible and in that way sharable, or, in other words, a physical representation of the text as transitional object.

One student, taken with the women in Ovid's *Metamorphoses* who were transformed into trees, used a project for her ceramics class to create a figure of one of those woman-trees breaking through the walls of a box that was attempting to constrain her. Her sculpture emphasized a tree's formidable strength in a way Ovid's text does not, and so presented an expansion of Ovid's viewpoint. Another student created a digital slide-show of photos of herself silhouetted against a sunset with her arms and face lifted toward the sky, images that were perplexing until the video's conclusion with the lines from Ovid's creation story about how the creatures with four legs must look downward while humans are made to hold their heads erect in majesty and see the sky and the stars. This student's re-envisioning of these words invested them with a weight and power easy to miss when they are encountered in the midst of Ovid's long text. A third student literally depicted himself in the imaginary world of the texts we read by placing images of himself, through a masterful use of Photoshop, into paintings of scenes from these texts. There on the deck of a ship with Odysseus tied to the mast, the ears of his crew bound, and sirens swarming, sits an image of my student, hands over his ears and face filled with terror. Producing creative projects like these requires of students a more thorough engagement with a literary work, whether that relationship best be described as inhabiting the world of the text or internalizing that text in order to transform it through their own perspective. Perhaps in such a state the reader is "in" the text as the text is at the same time "in" the reader. However it is articulated, the distance between reader and text temporarily disappears again and each affects the other. This second immersion in a literary work carries with it the insights gained from students' prior research and analysis. In addition, it takes on sharable form through these assignments, as students voice the words they've learned and present their creative projects in class, and we who experience the new works of art gain a new and illuminated vision of the text that inspired them.

Welcoming into the classroom students' own experiences of creating and entering into the imaginary worlds of the literary works on which a course focuses, using those experiences to motivate and direct inquiry into those texts, and inviting students to appropriate or "in-corporate" a literary work through memorization and re-creation do not guarantee that reading those works will become a formative experience for those students. But it will become a possibility. If reading literature indeed gives us opportunity to form and reform our sense of ourselves and our relation to the world around us and so can assist us, in Winnicott's words, with "the strain of relating inner and outer reality" (13), then it is imperative that we do what we can to open up for our students the possibility of using literary reading for the transformation of selves and cultures that is vital in our ever-changing world.

Works Cited

Agathocleous, Tanya, and Ann C. Dean, eds. *Teaching Literature: A Companion*. New York: Palgrave Macmillian, 2003.

Alter, Robert. *The Pleasures of Reading in an Ideological Age*. 1989. New York: Norton, 1996.

Altieri, Charles. "Taking Lyrics Literally: Teaching Poetry in a Prose Culture." *Teaching Literature: A Companion*. Ed. Tanya and Ann C. Dean Agathocleous. New York: Palgrave Macmillian, 2003. 80–101.

Appleman, Deborah. *Critical Encounters in High School English: Teaching Literary Theory to Adolescents*. New York: Teachers College Press, 2000.

Arbery, Glenn C. *Why Literature Matters: Permanence and the Politics of Reputation*. Wilmington, DE: ISI Books, 2001.

Arts, National Endowment for the. *Reading at Risk: A Survey of Literary Reading in America*. 2004. pdf. Available: http://arts.endow.gov/pub/ReadingAtRisk.pdf. June 16 2010.

Bamford, Karen, and Alexander Leggatt, eds. *Approaches to Teaching English Renaissance Drama*. New York: MLA, 2002.

Bialostosky, Don. "Should College English Be Close Reading?" *College English* 69.2 (2006): 111–16.

Bickman, Martin. *Minding American Education: Reclaiming the Tradition of Active Learning*. New York: Teachers College, 2003.

Blau, Sheridan. *The Literature Workshop: Teaching Texts and Their Readers*. Portsmouth, NH: Heinemann, 2003.

Bleich, David. "The Unconscious Troubles of Men." *Critical Theory and the Teaching of Literature: Politics, Curriculum, Pedagogy*. Eds. James F. Slevin and Art Young. Urbana, IL: NCTE, 1996. 47–62.

Bogdan, Deanne. *Re-Educating the Imagination: Toward a Poetics, Polititcs, and Pedagogy of Literary Engagement*. Portsmouth, NH: Boynton/Cook-Heinemann, 1992.

Bollas, Christopher. *Being a Character: Psychoanalysis and Self Experience*. New York: Hill and Wang, 1992.

Booth, Wayne C. *The Company We Keep: An Ethics of Fiction*. Berkeley: University of California Press, 1988.

Brooks, Cleanth. "Teaching 'the Love Song of J. Alfred Prufrock'." *Approaches to Teaching Eliot's Poetry and Plays*. Ed. Jewel Spears Brooker. New York: MLA, 1988. 78–87.

Bruner, Jerome. *Actual Minds, Possible Worlds*. Cambridge, MA: Harvard University Press, 1986.

Cavanagh, Sheila T. "Bringing Our Brains to the Humanities: Increasing the Value of Our Classes While Supporting Our Futures." *Pedagogy* 10.1 (2009): 131–42.

Clark, Miriam Marty. "Beyond Critical Thinking." *Pedagogy* 9.2 (2009): 325–30.

Collins, Billy. "The Companionship of a Poem." *The Chronicle of Higher Education* November 23, 2001.

Davis, Philip. *The Experience of Reading*. London: Routledge, 1992.

———. "The Place of the Implicit in Literary Discovery: Creating New Courses." *Teaching Literature: A Companion*. Eds. Tanya Agathocleous and Ann C. Dean. New York: Palgrave Macmillian, 2003. 149–62.

Donoghue, Denis. *The Practice of Reading*. New Haven, CT: Yale UP, 1998.

Edmundson, Mark. *Why Read?* New York: Bloomsbury, 2004.

Farrell, Frank B. *Why Does Literature Matter?* Ithaca, NY: Cornell University Press, 2004.

Felski, Rita. *Uses of Literature*. Malden, MA: Blackwell, 2008.

Gikandi, Simon. "Chinua Achebe and the Signs of the Times." *Approaches to Teaching Achebe's Things Fall Apart*. Ed. Bernth Lindfors. New York: MLA, 1991. 25–30.

Graff, Gerald. *Professing Literature: An Institutional History*. Chicago: University of Chicago Press, 1987.

Green, Daniel. "Abandoning the Ruins." *College English* 63 (2001): 273–87.

Guillory, John. *Cultural Capital: The Problem of Literary Canon Formation*. Chicago: University of Chicago Press, 1993.

Gumbrecht, Hans Ulrich. *Production of Presence: What Meaning Cannot Convey*. Stanford, CA: Stanford UP, 2004.

Haraway, Donna J. "Situated Knowledges: The Science Question in Feminism and the Privilege of Partial Perspective." *Simians, Cyborgs, and Women: The Reinvention of Nature*. New York: Routledge, 1991. 183–201.

Henry, Nancy. "Teaching the Victorians Today." *Teaching Literature: A Companion*. Eds. Tanya Agathocleous and Ann C. Dean. New York: Palgrave Macmillian, 2003. 49–57.

Iser, Wolfgang. *Prospecting: From Reader Response to Literary Anthropology*. Baltimore: Johns Hopkins UP, 1989.

Jusdanis, Gregory. *Fiction Agonistes: In Defense of Literature*. Stanford, CA: Stanford UP, 2010.

Lentricchia, Frank. "Last Will and Testament of an Ex-Literary Critic." *Lingua Franca* 6.6 (1996): 59–67.

Lewis, C. S. *An Experiment in Criticism*. Cambridge: Cambridge University Press, 1961.

Marshall, James D., Peter Smagorinsky, and Michael Smith. *The Language of Interpretation: Patterns of Discourse in Discussions of Literature*. Urbana, IL: NCTE, 1995.

McCormick, Kathleen, and Melissa Shofner. "Here Comes Everybody: An Epistemic Approach to Teaching *Ulysses* in a Small College." *Pedagogy* 10.2 (2010): 363–88.

McLemee, Scott. "The Grand Dame of Poetry Criticism." *The Chronicle of Higher Education* LI.21 (2005): A14–A16.

Mellor, Bronwyn, Annette Patterson, and Marnie O'Neill. *Reading Fictions: Applying Literary Theory to Short Stories*. 1991. Urbana, IL: NCTE-Chalkface, 2000.

——. *Reading Stories: Activities and Texts for Critical Readings*. 1987. Urbana, IL: NCTE-Chalkface, 2000.

Miller, J. Hillis. *On Literature*. New York: Routledge, 2002.

Miller, Richard E. "Schooling Misery: The Ominous Threat and the Eminent Promise of the Popular Reader." *Teaching Literature: A Companion*. Eds. Tanya Agathocleous and Ann C. Dean. New York: Palgrave MacMillian, 2003. 125–38.

Moody, A. D. "The Experience and the Meaning: *Ash-Wednesday*." *Approaches to Teaching Eliot's Poetry and Plays*. Ed. Jewel Spears Brooker. New York: MLA, 1988. 97–102.

Morson, Gary Saul. "Bakhtin and the Teaching of Literature." *Research in the Teaching of English* 41.3 (2007): 350–57.

O'Connor, Flannery. *Mystery and Manners*. Ed. Sally and Robert Fitzgerald. New York: Noonday Press, 1970.

O'Reilly, Meagan. Student Essay. Chapman U., 2008.

Ostovich, Helen. "'Our Sport Shall Be to Take What They Mistake': Classroom Performance and Learning." *Approaches to Teaching English Renaissance Drama*. Eds. Karen Bamford and Alexander Leggatt. New York: MLA, 2002. 87–94.

Perloff, Marjorie. *Differentials: Poetry, Poetics, Pedagogy*. Tuscaloosa: University of Alabama, 2004.

Purves, Alan C. "Toward a Reevaluation of Reader Response and School Literature." *Language Arts* 70 (1993): 348–61.

Ricoeur, Paul. *Freud and Philosophy: An Essay on Interpretation*. Trans. Denis Savage. New Haven: Yale University Press, 1970.

——. *From Text to Action: Essays in Hermeneutics, Ii*. Trans. Kathleen Blamey and John B. Thompson. Evanston, IL: Northwestern UP, 1991.

——. *Interpretation Theory: Discourse and the Surplus of Meaning*. Fort Worth, TX: Texas Christian University Press, 1976.

Roche, Mark William. *Why Literature Matters in the 21st Century*. New Haven: Yale University Press, 2004.

Rosenblatt, Louise. *Literature as Exploration*. 1938. 5th ed. New York: MLA, 1995.

——. *The Reader, the Text, the Poem: The Transactional Theory of the Literary Work*. 1978. Carbondale, IL: Southern Illinois University Press, 1994.

Scholes, Robert. *The Rise and Fall of English: Reconstructing English as a Discipline*. New Haven: Yale University Press, 1998.

——. *Textual Power: Literary Theory and the Teaching of English*. New Haven: Yale University Press, 1985.

Schwab, Gabriele. "Cultural Texts and Endopsychic Scripts." *SubStance: A Review of Theory and Literary Criticism* 30.94/95 (2001): 160–76.

——. *The Mirror and the Killer-Queen: Otherness in Literary Language.*
Bloomington, IN: Indiana University Press, 1996.

——. *Subjects without Selves: Transitional Texts in Modern Fiction.* Cambridge,
MA: Harvard University Press, 1994.

——. "Words and Moods: The Transference of Literary Knowledge."
SubStance: A Review of Theory and Literary Criticism 26.3 (1997): 107–27.

Scwhartz, Daniel R. *In Defense of Reading: Teaching Literature in the Twenty-
First Century.* Malden, MA: Wiley-Blackwell, 2008.

Seitz, James E. "How Literature Learns to Write: The Possibilities and
Pleasures of Role-Play." *Critical Theory and the Teaching of Literature:
Politics, Curriculum, Pedagogy.* Ed. James F. Slevin. Urbana, IL: NCTE,
1996. 328–40.

Showalter, Elaine. *Teaching Literature.* Malden, MA: Blackwell, 2003.

Slatoff, Walter J. *With Respect to Readers: Dimensions of Literary Response.*
Ithaca, NY: Cornel U P, 1970.

Spivak, Gayatri Chakravorty. "Uses of Levinas." Graduate Seminar.
University of California, Irvine, Spring 2004.

Sumara, Dennis J. *Why Reading Literature in School Still Matters: Imagination,
Interpretation, Insight.* Mahwah, NJ: Lawrence Erlbaum Associates, 2002.

Teague, Frances. "Responding to Renaissance Drama: One Way of Guiding
Students." *Approaches to Teaching English Renaissance Drama.* Eds. Karen
Bamford and Alexander Leggatt. New York: MLA, 2002. 63–72.

Tompkins, Jane. *A Life in School: What the Teacher Learned.* Cambridge, MA:
Perseus Books, 1996.

Traoré, Ousseynou. "Matrical Approach to *Things Fall Apart.*" *Approaches to
Teaching Achebe's Things Fall Apart.* Ed. Bernth Lindfors. New York: MLA,
1991. 65–73.

Waller, Gary. "Polylogue: Ways of Teaching and Structuring the Conflicts."
Critical Theory and the Teaching of Literature: Politics, Curriculum, Pedagogy.
Eds. James F. Slevin and Art Young. Urbana, IL: NCTE, 1996. 189–206.

Waller, Gary, Kathleen McCormick, and Lois Josephs Fowler. *The Lexington
Introduction to Literature: Reading and Responding to Texts.* Lexington, MA:
D. C. Heath, 1987.

Wilhelm, Jeffrey D. *"You Gotta Be the Book": Teaching Engaged and Reflective
Reading with Adolescents.* Language and Literacy Series. New York:
Teachers College Press, 1997.

Williams, Carolyn. "Teaching Autobiography." *Teaching Literature: A
Companion.* Eds. Tanya Agathocleous and Ann C. Dean. New York:
Palgrave MacMillian, 2003. 11–30.

Winnicott, D. W. *Playing and Reality.* London: Tavistock, 1971.

Zunshine, Lisa. *Why We Read Fiction: Theory of Mind and the Novel.*
Columbus, OH: Ohio State University Press, 2006.

Index

CPSIA information can be obtained
at www.ICGtesting.com
Printed in the USA
LVHW020959130721
692566LV00009B/728